CATAPULT THE COW

Gary Conner

Catapult the Cow

ISBN-13: 978-1461065968

ISBN-10: 1461065968

Author: Gary B Conner

            3530 North Coast Hwy

            Newport, OR 97365

            503-580-1156 (phone)

            Lean1mfg@aol.com (email)

            www.lean1mfg.com (website)

            or: www.catapultthecow.com

Editing Services Provided by: Kristi Smith

Dedicated to:

My Creator; for the gift of life...

...and to Pamela, for sharing her life with me.

Table of Contents

Chapter	Title	Page

Acknowledgement

This is a story book.

These are stories of the places I've been, the companies I've worked with, and the people I've met. The stories presented here are now metabolized into my DNA. Every experience and every person I've ever worked with have been indelibly impressed into my memory. You might say that the synapses in my brain have been permanently rewired by the teams and individuals detailed in the stories that follow.

My fondest memories as a child were listening to my grandfather tell his stories. I guess that I am a story teller too. People often tell me that the stories I tell during my seminars are the best part of the workshop for them. In this book I hope to capture some of the best stories I have.

Most of the stories are short, but I hope you can find a message or moral in each one. My writing is neither grandiose nor poetic. I want this book to sound like a conversation. I hope to relate these stories as I would (and have) with friends over a cup of coffee.

I am a shop floor guy, and I wanted to write this for other shop floor guys. There are plenty of high tech books, complete with their seventy-five cent words, written by highly educated people from the halls of academia (not that there's anything wrong with that).

This book is not meant to compete with them, and I can't hope to do so. This book is not meant to sit in the reference section of a technical library. I would be happier to see dog-eared copies of this book littering lunch room tables or sitting proudly atop toilet tanks in company restrooms; where people could read a short story during their daily meditation.

This is my fifth book on the subject of process improvement. I am very excited about this text because it provides me the opportunity to share some of the experiences and stories I've had from working with hundreds of kaizen teams and thousands of unforgettable people.

What a privilege I've had to have shared my working life helping others to make their working lives better.

I have too many people to thank to try to write a traditional acknowledgement, so I will simply say "thank you!" to all the kaizen team members who worked so hard to catapult the cow (you will understand after chapter one).

These teams have achieved amazing results, by looking *inward* for solutions, stretching far beyond their comfort zone, examining their current condition, questioning time tested processes, and challenging each other and themselves (not an easy thing to do).

These teams no doubt lost copious amounts of sleep, but in the process generated innumerable ideas; most of which completely blew me away.

By means of their common sense, intelligence, energies, talent, creativity, willingness, trust in the process and *in me,* they made my job as facilitator meaningful for the companies we were trying to help, and personally rewarding for me. I hope that the experiences have meant as much for the individual team members as they have for me.

Thank you all!

Chapter One

Catapult the cow

The scene in Monty Python's movie *Search for the Holy Grail* where inhabitants of a castle catapult a cow toward an invading military force is familiar to many. However, most people are unaware that it is based on an *actual event* documented as having happened in the 14th Century. In 1334, Margartea Maultasch (of Tyrol) had her army invade the small kingdom in Carinthia.

Illustration 1.1 Margartea Maultasch Source: www.wikipedia.com

Her forces encircled the castle of Hochosterwitz. Viewing the photograph of the castle makes it clear why the invaders could not storm the walls as they normally might.

Because of the terrain, a traditional attack of the castle was out of the question. After the small kingdom's local population ran into the fortress and barred the doors, the invaders decided that it would be easiest to wait them out. Their thought was "We will simply starve out the inhabitants."

The situation inside the castle was desperate; supplies were scarce and they were soon down to their last two bags of grain, and one skinny cow.

The commander of the castle took desperate action. He slaughtered the cow and filled it with the grain, ordering his troops to catapult the dead cow over the wall toward the enemy. The invading hordes interpreted this as a clear message that starving them out was useless; obviously they had food to waste. The invaders picked up and moved on.

Illustration 1.2   Hochosterwitz   Source: www.wikipedia.com

What does this have to do with business in America? Over the past few years we have seen millions of US jobs lost. Our economy is still in a precarious position after what looked like an impending implosion. Only time will tell if the exhaustive efforts and billions of dollars applied in the hopes of shoring up our once powerful financial engine will prove successful.

Unless we apply significant and radical changes to the approach we take to business (and manufacturing) we will continue to see ourselves *starved out* (like those in the castle mentioned at the outset) by invading competition.

Times have changed. After World War II the manufacturing capabilities of the rest of the world had for the most part been dismantled, destroyed, or modified to support the war effort. Our parents and grandparents had the markets cornered. The US was one of the few countries where manufacturing capability was still intact. Customers were beating down the doors of our parents' businesses to get product manufactured.

That condition has changed dramatically. It is now a "me too" marketplace. In the current environment, we compete with countries who have not only rebuilt their manufacturing capabilities, but have done so using techniques like *Lean Manufacturing* and *Six Sigma;* based on systems developed by Japanese manufacturers.

Foreign competitors may have the additional advantage of paying significantly lower wages and providing little or no benefits. They may also be ignoring the long term cost associated with unsafe working conditions or environmental concerns. All of this contributes to an unlevel playing field.

In order to compete responsibly we cannot lower our safety standards, diminish our concern for the environment, or hope to retain skilled team members without rewarding them appropriately; but we do have to do something.

We have to end the *We versus Them*, management-labor relationships. We have to eliminate the old school *economic order quantity, bigger is better* mentality that has poisoned business logic over the past six decades.

As Monty Python would say, "now for something completely different!"

Illustration 1.3 Monty Python   Source: New Media Broadcasting Company, Inc.

We have had thirty years to learn from Honda, Toyota, John Deere, Pella Windows and other world class companies. We need to study their transformations. We need to adapt our financial, marketing, sales, order entry, purchasing, scheduling, manufacturing, and delivery systems.

Unfortunately, the vast majority of US companies stubbornly refuse to acknowledge that there could be a better way. Some take the stance that "The current process was good enough for Dad and Granddad, it's good enough for us!"

World Class (Lean) Manufacturing is no longer an option. And it doesn't apply just to the "shop" or only to manufacturing. The entire enterprise must adopt these principles, and soon.

We may have to *catapult the cow*; try something difficult and unexpected in order to get the result we want. We are not recommending that anyone throw their entire company over the wall as if there is no hope.

We *are,* however, suggesting that you begin transforming to the Lean approach. Begin with a model line. Identify 20-25% of your company (a significant percentage), and begin applying the Lean Manufacturing principles. Start small, but start!

Our message and warning to all manufacturers is this: There is no *ideal* or *easy* time to start. But this is sure: "If you wait six months you will be six months further behind."

Recent effort by governments to bail out floundering banking systems and auto manufacturing companies was like handing out money to compulsive gamblers. Dr. Phil said it best: "You cannot solve money problems with money!" When an individual is inclined to overspend and squander limited resources, providing them "handout" money can only serve to enable the bad behavior.

If the problem we were dealing with were actually about compulsive gambling, I'm sure that the government's solution would not be to stand out in front of a casino handing out hundred dollar bills. Doubtless, the solution would include a plan to rehabilitate the addicted gamblers. Our entire country must be rehabilitated to think in a completely new way; to recognize the cause and effect of each action we take, and determine if each action is *value added* or not.

For decades (in manufacturing) we have been taught that we must build and stockpile large quantities of product; using shared resources, huge machines and costly tracking systems in order to cover the cost of enormous set-up times on complicated equipment. World class companies are showing us that there is a different path. Smaller lot sizes, right-sized equipment, smaller value-stream structure, visual signals, quicker set-ups, and higher velocity requiring little or no tracking have proven to be a more financially attractive and robust method.

Lean Manufacturing is not rocket science. It is a set of basic tools that provide a systematic and repeatable process to identify and eliminate waste. The challenge within *make-to-order* companies is to adapt world class techniques in high-mix, low-volume environments.

The manufacturing disciplines utilized by our parents and grandparents are no longer a viable approach. Einstein said it best, "The definition of insanity is to repeat the same process and expect a different result." Many organizations continue to practice (and educational institutions continue to teach) manufacturing principles that worked for our forefathers, while ignoring the fact that the playing field has changed significantly.

Some remain stubbornly unconvinced of the value of modifying past behaviors, like typewriter manufacturers doggedly trying to hold onto the past during the introduction of personal computers.

We must examine our current processes every day and challenge whether they continue to be an economically viable approach.

It is rare these days to come across companies who have totally ignored the message to adopt Lean techniques. Most companies have flirted with a technique or two, (e.g.: scrap reduction, 5-S or Set-up reduction) and some have even attempted a Lean transformation.

However, due to the *firefight* of running and growing a business, these companies frequently struggle to sustain the gains. That struggle to sustain has led some of those companies to abandon the change because the techniques applied at companies like Toyota seem unreasonable within smaller business models where *high-mix, low-volume* sales patterns are the norm. In the process, they *short sell* the idea of spending time looking for waste.

Illustration 1.4 Shigeo Shingo   Source: LSS Acadamy

15

Mr. Shingo of the Toyota Motor Works described seven primary forms of waste. We have since identified even more, all of which can have a negative impact on both the bottom line and on the environment.

1. Transportation waste
2. Waste of motion
3. Waiting
4. Over-production
5. Defects
6. Excessive processing
7. Inventory

One of the mistakes we have seen some companies make is *shot-gunning* their transformation. They perform a 5-S event in one area, a set-up reduction in another; they experiment with a kanban replenishment system in a totally different area and attempt to improve plant layout in yet another.

Years later they often express frustration at the lack of progress and sustainment. We recommend that our clients totally transform a small part of the business; first by identifying their value streams, selecting one, and then transforming it into a *Model Line.*

In doing so, they minimize what has become known as *Kamakazi Kaizen* events. Sadly, some companies measure the success of their continuous improvement program by how many kaizen events they conduct in a year. It has been said "you cannot kaizen your way to world class." You must be good at finishing, not just at starting projects. The number of events is less important than the quality of the outcome. What is of critical importance is asking the question: "will the project result in improved product or information flow?"

By using the concept of a model line, teams avoid developing a Lean Manufacturing system that lacks depth or which seems like a brittle veneer. We encourage teams to drill to the "bedrock" and firmly establish the appropriate tools within the model line, quantify the benefits, and justify (and fund) future events. In doing so, they overcome resistance and quickly spread best practices and lessons learned to other value streams.

There is a common theme among the most successful teams; they tend to focus on how each idea or recommendation will impact the flow of *value* to the customer. They also avoid starting in the middle of the process where an improvement causes the product or delivery of service to simply hurry up and wait longer.

By starting as close to the customer as possible products are ready to sell earlier. Customers are able to recognize the improvements in the form of reduced lead times.

This text will relate just a sampling of the stories, case studies, and examples of individuals and companies doing the *hard* thing, the *unexpected* thing. I hope to inspire you to do the same. In hindsight, I wish I would have kept a better diary. I have met so many interesting characters in my travels.

I've been blessed to have had the opportunities to spend time with teams in nearly every industry, at every educational level, and in a wide range of technology:

From log truck drivers and crane operators sorting freshly cut trees on a log deck in Willamina, Oregon, to scientists designing and producing new medical devices to save lives.

From a steel mill; grinding and melting scrap cars on one end of the process and shooting out construction re-bar from the other end; to a silicon gasket manufacturer producing parts for the aerospace customers, including the space shuttle.

I've worked with companies involved in food processing, primary and secondary wood, primary and secondary metals, glass, plastics, administrative processes, engineering, foundries, railcar remanufacturing. You name it, I've seen it. It is the best job in the world, and I can think of nothing I would rather do!

And I just love manufacturing. I work on the road all week and when I get home my twelve year old son and I end up watching "How it's Made", or "Made in America", or some other show describing the innovative nature of mankind. I can't get enough of it! I hope to share just a few of my most favorite memories (good and bad) in the hope of assisting others toward their world class vision, and to help them avoid pitfalls along their journey.

The results of some of these stories are amusing, some a little scary, others are breathtaking, and some are just for fun. In every case my goal is to help fill your *sail* with wind; to encourage, enthuse and motivate you to stay on the path toward your goal of world class performance.

Without exception there is always a time when the hard work and the *concrete heads* will have you second guessing your resolve. You will need encouragement. Just as in life we hit speed bumps and detours that temporarily take us off track. Sometimes we need that *wake-up call* from a trusted friend to say: "Hey where are you? I thought you were on the path!"

At times that wake-up call comes in the form a story from a person unknown to us; maybe a fifteen second sound bite on CNN about a homeless man who earlier in life had thrown away his life to drugs. We see his desperate situation turned around because someone reaches out to him. We see him splashed on every TV screen and magazine as he is given a second chance. We are transfixed as we watch him in one moment taking advantage and thriving in a restored life while the next moment he is wrestling with demons from his past.

We empathetically hope the best for him in his journey to restore a life once shattered, understanding that no one can make life's decisions for him.

That's why reality shows work. We are people watchers. Regardless of the outcome, we are easily engaged by watching or hearing about the life experiences of our fellow humans. We are instinctively interested. And we are often profoundly affected by the experiences of others.

We may read a story that restores our faith in others and within ourselves, think: "Chicken Soup for the Soul". It is my hope that this book becomes a kind of: "Fat-free Soup for the Lean Manufacturers Soul".

We all need encouragement from time to time, me included. Sometimes in the midst of a particularly difficult project I reach a point of frustration and discouragement. I'll find myself struggling to maintain a positive attitude, then I will remember the story of Kurt and how he marked out his body on the concrete floor with blue masking tape during a 5-S event (full story to follow); and a smile will explode across my face as I realize that as difficult as the problem I am facing might be, there will simply be *that much more* satisfaction when we finally reach the finish line!

Between Lean, Six Sigma, Theory of Constraints, Total Quality Management, and other disciplines I count over 160 distinct tools (in addition to countless variations) in what I could call the collective World Class Manufacturing practioner's toolbox. I can't hope to provide examples of each one in this format, but I hope to share examples of many of the fundamental and most important tools and techniques as possible in the form of stories.

I want to reinforce the idea early on that these techniques do not apply solely to manufacturing. Service-oriented businesses are also successfully adopting these same tools. I have even worked with governmental agencies in the US and Canada, including the immigration department in one Province of Canada, as well as the Canadian counterpart to our Department of Human Services; helping them to expedite assistance to those needing financial or legal aide, equipment like wheelchairs, or other medical assistance.

While they are not *for profit* organizations, they do have budgets, so the tools and techniques in the Lean toolbox have proven equally effective in reducing costs and streamlining processes as they work to serve their constituents; just as traditional manufactures try to meet the needs of their customers.

There are a few sectors of our economy that seem to have held back, and my hope is that by means of these stories I might raise awareness in new demographics as well; the airline industry, rental car, hotel, restaurant industry, medical services … on and on….

Every contributor to every segment of our economy needs to develop the culture and mentality that there *has* to be a better way, a more 'value added' method to deliver product or service. Our offshore competitors are sure to find it because "necessity is the mother of invention."

While our foreign competition may have plentiful and low-cost labor resources available to them, they generally have less access to raw materials, space (land), technology, transportation systems, and other resources that we may take for granted. Our competition is *forced* to think outside the box, while many companies in the US have remained locked *inside* their box; a box often created by ourselves; a self induced prison of stagnated thought.

Just because 'big batch-push system' processes worked for our forefathers, does not mean that they are viable approaches for us or our children as we operate in a new economic generation.

Chapter Two

Kurt's Outline

It was just a few short weeks after the horrific events of 9/11/2001. Everyone was still distracted and, understandably, still in shock. The economy was beginning to recoil, suffering blowback from the terror attacks and just ahead of the housing bubble implosion yet to come. My phone had been quiet for weeks and I was starting to panic like I always do when the phone is quiet. Then, like a dark cloud lifting, a local Oregon machine shop called to ask if I provided 5-S training (a technique of workspace organization).

I was ecstatic; partly because of the work, partly because I didn't have to get on an airplane. I took a tour of their plant and we identified a target area; a tool room shared by thirty five machinists. I met with their team which included the tool room manager. He was a rather diminutive five foot, three inch tall gentleman of advancing years. He sported a well trimmed beard minus the mustache and wore what looked to me to be traditional mantles of someone from Pennsylvania Dutch heritage; he looked like he would have been completely comfortable driving a horse drawn buggy. His thick glasses and jewelers loop (for inspecting tools at close range) made for a unique picture inside a shop full of burly Oregon machinists!

I worked with the management team to scope out the project and then I went about generating a proposal. We came to an agreement and set a date to start the project a few weeks later on a crisp November morning.

I was setting up the training room as the team filed in one after another. We were going to train about a dozen people the first day and then split off with four or five kaizen (a term that means continuous improvement) team members to actually carry out the balance of the five day project. As we always do, we would gather together the management team, and all those affected by the kaizen on Friday afternoon. Our end of week presentation would provide them a summary; a report explaining the team's findings , recommendations, new best practices, and costs and benefits analysis.

But this was Monday morning, the first day of training, and as I awaited the arrival of our final team member (the tool room supervisor) the group was getting anxious to start. I don't believe in punishing people for being on time, so I asked "Should we wait for Kurt, or should we get started?" They looked at each other and someone responded, "oh, Kurt won't be on the kaizen event."

My state of surprise must have been apparent to the group because they stuttered for few moments and looked to their group leader to provide an explanation. He felt the pressure of all eyes on him and finally offered, "Kurt is two years away from retirement. He said that we could do anything we want to in the tool room, but he just wants to be left out of this event. Is that a problem?"

I would ordinarily not take a project where the key player appeared to be so resistant. I did not find it encouraging to realize on day one of the event that the 'owner' of the process was obviously *checked out*. Had I have known that information prior to the start of the project I may have chosen to *no bid* the request for proposal.

To be honest with myself, with the lack of work in my consulting backlog at the time I probably would have opted to give it a try anyway! Hindsight being a perfect 20/20, I am certainly glad I chose to continue with the project.

After the initial training and a workplace scan of the target area, I wondered to myself if our plan was too aggressive . The tool room occupied an area roughly 30 feet square (900 square feet) with some additional small rooms that had been tagged on at random over the years of constant growth. Seven tool cabinets, each with ten or twelve drawers, were chock-a-block full of milling and lathe tooling. There may have been a sense of order Kurt's mind, but no one else could put a finger on it. If a machinist needed to retrieve a tool (e.g.: 3/8" end mill) and Kurt happened to be unavailable, it was anyone's guess where the required tool might be stored.

When machinists were finished with one work order they would come to the tool room to retrieve paperwork, tooling, and set-up equipment for their next job. They would drop off tooling from the previous job on any open surface. Every table, every desk, every cart, every shelf, and every drawer was completely covered in litter, broken tools, new tools still in the package, old tools waiting to be put away or sent out for repair, along with sample parts, fixtures, clamps, paperwork and while I never found out why; a chain saw blade (see illustration)!

I did not sleep well that Monday night. Had I bitten off too big a bite? Scoping out a project is probably one of the most important aspects of the proposal. It's like you are marking off the project area with Police tape; in essence, saying we are going to work *here*, but not *there*. We certainly had our work cut out for us, especially considering Kurt's lack of participation.

Tuesday was spent on the first of the five S's; Sort. We *sorted* out everything that was deemed unnecessary to the day to day operation of an effective tool room. We used the 'red-tag' process to identify, store and disposition hundreds of items (including the chain saw blade).

By mid week we had identified the items that *were* required. We brainstormed a new filing system for the storage, replenishment, and retrieval of tooling. We began organizing (Straightening) the area so that anyone could find anything within thirty seconds (we call this the thirty second test).

Most 5-S practitioners count Straighten as the second of the five techniques, but in talking to the original translator of the Toyota program, we have found that Shine is actually the second "S" when you are performing the 5-S's for the first time in an area. This makes sense when you think about it; why would you ever bring in a dirty item to a work area? *Sort, Shine, Straighten* the first time, *Sort, Straighten, Shine* every day after the initial event.

So everything was organized and we created visual indicators and written documentation to identify tooling. We set up point of use storage locations for consumable items like sandpaper and cutting fluids, putting them on a visual replenishment program commonly referred to as a kanban system.

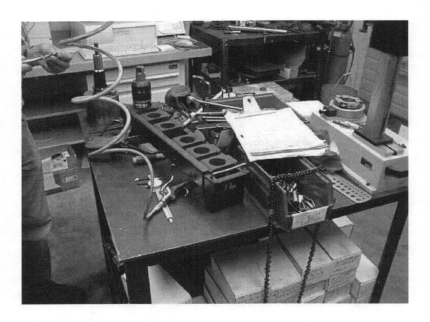

Illustration 2.1   "Before" Condition in Machine Shop Tool Room

This satisfied the *Standardization* requirement of the 5-S program. Now anyone could find a tool, not just Kurt!

The kaizen team recommended that the company implement an audit program to ensure that the last S in the 5-S program: *Sustainment* would be possible and expected.

Despite my earlier fears, and in spite of the tool room manager's lack of participation, we were successful in accomplishing our team objectives by noon on Friday. That achievement required a few late hours and extra effort by the kaizen team, but the team was committed to see it through. There was a still a *thirty day list* of items needing attention like buying new carts and other things that were outside the authority of the team, but for the most part the project was a great success.

Illustration 2.2   "Before" Condition in Machine Shop Tool Room

My work there was done. The only thing left to do would be to develop and deliver the end of week kaizen presentation.

As the team was gathered up our tools and materials Kurt approached me. Imagine my surprise! I had not seen or heard much of anything from Kurt all week, so it was a bit overwhelming to see him standing there holding out his hand. He asked "can I borrow your blue tape?"

I stopped short, pulling the roll of blue masking tape back out of the kaizen tool box. We had been using the blue tape to temporarily mark out cart locations, mask paint lines on the floor, or to show work flow direction and identify other tool room details all week long.

27

Naturally, I handed the tape over to Kurt with a self satisfied smile; thinking to myself, "maybe Kurt is finally getting it!"

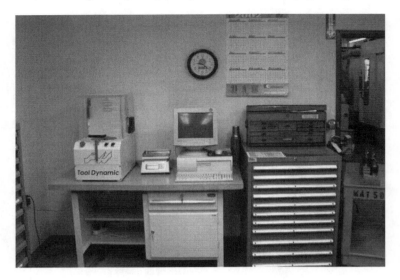

Illustration 2.3   "After" Condition in Machine Shop Tool Room

The kaizen team celebrated with a pizza lunch while we generated the presentation that we would deliver to the entire shop. We attached *before and after* photographs to flip charts, and we drew up visual descriptions of how to find any tool in any cabinet within 30 seconds.

We heard the shop intercom calling everyone to the tool room precisely at 1:00 pm. The kaizen team gave one last nervous look to each other as we picked up our easels, flip charts, and other presentation materials and headed downstairs to the tool room.

We approached the completely transformed tool room, now filled with people so that there was standing room only for the

35 machinists. We couldn't help but notice that everyone's gaze seemed completely transfixed on the concrete floor before them.

As we parted the crowd to set up our flip charts and easels, the subject of their attention became apparent. In our absence, Kurt had used the blue masking tape to draw the outline of a body on the concrete floor. It looked like an outline of his body! Everyone in the kaizen team recoiled and stopped in their tracks.

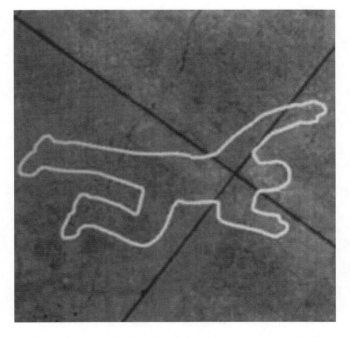

Illustration 2.4   Chalk outline (similar to Kurt's tape outline)

I thought to myself "oh, no! What is Kurt up to? This is going to ruin everything."

The shock I felt had to be apparent on my face, but I just shook it off and told myself, "no! We can't let this distract from the great work that this kaizen team just accomplished. "

"Just don't look directly at it!" I thought to myself.

The team followed my lead, and we just ignored the blue image on the floor. The presentation took about 15 minutes, and if head nodding was any indication, everyone seemed very impressed with the results. I then asked if anyone had anything to add; questions or comments. We fielded a few questions which took an additional ten minutes or so. I asked again "any other comments?"

Wouldn't you know it...Kurt was standing in the back of the room with his arm in the air. I took a deep breath, smiled my most convincing smile, and invited Kurt's comment. He stepped to the front of the room right in front of our flip chart. He turned and silently stared at the *before and after* photos for what seemed an eternity, but was in reality more like a few seconds. He turned back to the audience of 35 machinists and said: "I will be honest. I was not happy about this kaizen event in my area. But now that I see the results, (he pointed to the photographs) I see how this is going to make everyone's job easier, including mine. This team did some amazing things in four days."

He paused, "and if anyone ever comes in here and makes my tool-room look like this again (he turned and pointed to the *before* picture)...then you will look like this!" And he swung his pointed finger toward the tape outline sprawled out on the floor. Everyone broke into a nervous laugh. I breathed a sigh of relief!

In the end I think Kurt *did* get it. He realized that the kaizen process made his working life better. When I had originally showed up, his peers suggested that Kurt was two years away from retirement and couldn't wait for the day he could leave. I was back four years later and he was still there, happy and healthy. That's exactly what kaizen, 5-S, or any world class technique should do; it should make people's lives better.

I might add that when I visited the company years later, I had to comment that Kurt had sustained the transformed tool room's 5-S conditions better than anyone I had ever worked with to that point in my career. The team worked hard to achieve the improvements, and the behaviors of everyone involved had to be modified if sustainment was going to have a chance. This company (and Kurt), continue to serve as an example for all of us.

Chapter Three

"Have a nice day"

My first visit to DEP was scheduled to perform an assessment and offer suggestions to their management team about adopting Lean manufacturing processes within their 'lost wax investment casting' business.

If you have never been inside a lost wax casting plant, you would be amazed at the blend of high technology and what I can only describe as brute force manufacturing!

The process starts with small pellets of wax that are melted and forced into a mold. This molded wax will later be melted away to provide a 'cavity' in which metal will replace wax inside a mold; becoming a final product such as an artificial knee or replacement hip. A number of these small wax molds are then locked (melted) together onto a larger mold along with up to twenty other such products.

The entire mold (now about the size of a passenger car wheel) is dipped into a slurry of ceramic soup, then a twenty foot tall robot manipulates the entire mold under what looks like a waterfall of sand. This builds up a crust on the mold that is then dried in a climate controlled room for a number of hours. This process of dipping and applying sand is repeated up to ten times after which the mold begins to look like the bottom of your shoes after a long walk in a clay bog.

In one room they were X-raying delicate titanium (or cobalt) medical products that look more like chrome sculptures. These components would find their way to hospitals and would soon be placed into a human body. On the other side of the wall, a team of three men carried out a carefully choreographed dance; looking very much like space men or robots walking around in shimmering silver suits that were designed to protect them from the heat of 2500° gas-fired ovens. These special suits allow them to reach directly into pre-heat ovens to retrieve the sand impregnated molds. They then literally and physically run the white-hot, glowing casting across the room and place it into a shallow pit of sand. After that, they quickly and manually wrestle a 2700° crucible of molten cobalt into place over the mold; still nearly transparent from the pre-heating process.

Once the mold is pulled from the oven, they have less than 15 seconds to pour the 10 pound average crucible of liquid metal. If this 15 second limit is exceeded, the ambient oxygen in the room will draw into the mold, spoiling the casting with porosity, cracks, and air pockets. Repair is impossible at that point since impurities, air pockets, cracks and other defects would render the metal unsuitable for transplant into a patient.

Any mistakes at this point would require them to start the process completely over; resulting in days or weeks of lost effort.

As you can imagine, my first experience and visit to this casting plant was an exciting one; intriguing, and a bit scary, as glowing bits of molten material rained down around us during our tour of the casting department!

It was equally surprising to sit in the General Manager's office and listen to the very 'prescriptive' nature of their Lean manufacturing vision. They had already talked to other Lean manufacturing consultants and were very clear that they were looking for something extremely specific.

I believe his exact words were something like: "It seems like everything we've read about Lean manufacturing has to do with moving equipment around into physical 'cells'. We are not going to do that."

He looked at me as though he was waiting for some kind of reaction. Then he continued, "we are not going to put a 2,500° pre-heating oven next to a wax press, and we are not going to drop a half-million dollar X-ray machine into a dirty investing department where sand is being blown around by hurricane-force mold drying fans." He paused again, squinting a little this time; surveying my facial expression for the slightest hint of disagreement.

Recognizing none, he leaned forward in his chair, interlocked his fingers as he placed his hands on the table between us, and then, as if preparing to dismiss me, he summarized: "So..." (long pause) "...we'd like to take a shot at this lean manufacturing thing, but we are not Toyota. If your solution involves moving equipment... then it has been very nice to meet you!"

I pride myself on not being dogmatic about the application of the Toyota model. I grew up in a job shop, and we struggled with adopting some of the tools that were applied at Toyota. On the other hand, I have seen many people argue that "Lean manufacturing won't work here!" and we have proven otherwise. I was willing to give it a try, even with the caveat (mandate) that no equipment would be moved.

Long story short, we value stream mapped the process (about 50 distinct steps), we brainstormed alternatives and ideas for improvement, and the results were breathtaking.

Their current state was providing a 41 day lead time, at one hundred molds per day that equated to 4,100 molds in process. With a sales value of approximately $1,000 per mold, they had $4,100,000 tied up in 'work-in-process' inventory.

At the end of the 16-day event (4four-day kaizen events spread over three months) we had reduced lead time from 41 days to just over 12 days; seven days of which were to transfer the product to the Mid-West (United States) for heat treating. Their 'in-plant' process time could now be measured in hours rather than in weeks!

They freed up $2.9 million of inventory and quality improved substantially. My work there was complete! We celebrated, we ate cake, we slapped each other on the back, and we parted company.

I went on to work with other clients and felt good about the improvements; more confident than ever about the Lean manufacturing tools we used, especially considering the fact that we were not permitted to physically move any machinery into work cells.

It was about 6 months later that my cell phone rang, and I was a bit surprised to see that the number on caller ID was DEP Corp. "Uh oh, what's wrong?" I thought. It was the General Manager. "Good morning Dick!" I cheerily sang out.

Illustration 3.1   "Before" condition plant layout (spaghetti diagram)

We exchanged pleasantries for a couple of minutes and then came the inevitable few seconds of silence as I waited for him to address the reason for his call. He stammered a little, "you know...remember when...You know how, when we got rid of all that inventory?" He was searching for the right words "Well...all that space that used to be filled up with inventory...it's all empty space now." He paused "We can't keep moving this material so far between processes." Finally, he got to the point, "we need to move the furniture." I tried not to smile, even though I knew he couldn't see me. He and his team had finally determined (on their own) that moving the equipment was possible (and necessary) given their improved 'Lean' processes. So again, I was contracted to assist them in achieving the next level on their journey to World Class status.

That project was equally successful! They even got some national exposure based on the results of their efforts. They became recognized in their industry as a leader. Soon afterward, a large international holding company swooped in and bought them up. Within two years, an even larger company swooped in and bought them from *the first* holding company.

Illustration 3.2 "After" condition plant layout (spaghetti diagram)

As we began our plant layout efforts, we developed a visual representation of the product flow for each value stream by overlaying yarn on a three dimensional scale model of their plant. The results were a continuous length of yarn that measured 112 feet long. Each inch of yarn represented 12 feet (a total travel distance of over 16,000 feet per mold).

After the project, the new layout resulted in a yarn length of only 6 feet (less than 900 feet of travel distance per mold)!

Prior to their Lean efforts they were a small fish in a big pond; money was tight and competition was fierce. Now they have established themselves as an industry leader and they are also experiencing consistent growth and profits. They have the benefits associated with the deeper pockets of a parent company; providing job security for their teams, team families, and community. In the process, US manufacturing has become much stronger because of their leadership.

The last time I visited the General Manager's office there was a framed letter hanging on the wall. He walked me over to the letter, obviously proud of it, and waited while I read it. It was addressed to his company from their largest customer. In so many words, it read: "If you keep doing what you are doing, we have no choice but to buy from you!" Can you imagine a buyer writing such a letter to their supplier?

There was a condition though, "*If* you keep doing what you are doing..." *What* they have been doing is *cutting lead time by nearly 75%*, being able to *reduce costs* because they have eliminated nearly $3 million dollars of inventory, they have *improved quality* because if they have reason to suspect that a quality problem has made its way into their value stream, there are only 1,200 potentially suspect molds in process instead of the previous number of 4,100.

All these factors make it very difficult for the customer to go anywhere else to get the same level of performance in quality, cost, and delivery.

Quality, cost, and delivery; these three issues are the key decision drivers utilized by customers as they decide how to obtain needed products or services. In large part, our ability to satisfy these needs determines our ability to maintain customer loyalty.

DEP has met these criteria to a degree that most competitors in their industry cannot hope to emulate. That is, unless they begin to adopt World Class and Lean manufacturing techniques as well.

Chapter Four

Curt's cat

I live in Newport, on the beautiful Central Oregon coast. One of my clients is in the Astoria area, a historic town on the Northern Oregon coast.

While the geographic features and history of that area would certainly be considered breathtaking by most people, I'm not sure I would call it beautiful! They probably have their share of nice days; I've just never been there when that was the case.

Many people refer to this area as the Wet Coast (as opposed to West Coast). In addition to the rain, it is windy, foggy, and dreary a good percentage of the time.

Astoria has the un-enviable position of being located between the Pacific Ocean, with the accompanying weather effects common to that body of water, and the mouth of the Columbia River Gorge, which at times seems to generate its own weather systems.

The Gorge often acts as a funnel for scouring out cold winds from all points east including Mount Hood and her Cascade Brothers and Sisters, and directing frigid winds, ice storms, and other brutal weather features straight toward Astoria.

My client makes agricultural equipment here. They produce a machine that grinds up and packs alfalfa and other grasses in long bags, allowing the storage of feed for cattle and horses right in the field; as opposed to typical baling systems which require farmers to move the hay to a storage location and then back into the fields as feed is needed.

After the peak growing season, huge combines fill 40 foot dump trucks which then back up to the machine, depositing their loads of alfalfa. The machine grinds the grass and fills the bag like a five hundred foot long sausage. The 8 foot tall, 500 foot long bratwurst is left behind in the field, peeled back like a banana throughout the grass' dormant winter months, providing the animals a rich diet of nearly fresh alfalfa.

The company's sales demand requires one machine be produced every fourteen days. This was probably the longest *takt time* (rate of production) I had ever seen.

In addition to a number of engineers, stock room personnel, and kitting teams, 5 people were primarily responsible to assemble this behemoth machine. One of the 5 assemblers was Curt. Curt's responsibility was to fabricate, weld, and assemble what they called the 'tunnel extension'. This extension was where the farmer would hang the unfurled 500 foot long bag. As you can see in the photograph in illustration 4.1, floor space was limited, so Curt did his work in an outbuilding; really little more than a lean-to. This lean-to provided no heat, inadequate lighting, no companionship or company except a feral cat who had taken up residence in one corner the shed. For months, Curt shared his sandwiches with the cat in an effort to nurture the only working relationship he had.

Needless to say, Curt's working life was not a comfortable one. Because of his location (outside the main shop) he was not permitted frequent interaction with his team mates. He was

41

isolated; he was cold in the winter time; he sweltered in the 90% plus humidity of summer.

He was left to work in little better than a fog encased shack nine months out of the year. For all these reasons Curt was not happy. His only source of joy seemed to be the stray cat and chain smoking, (by the way, in an effort to minimize loneliness the war department provided cigarettes to soldiers during World War I and II).

Illustration 4.1 "Before" condition 5-S project

I spent a number of days there spread over a number of months. We applied many Lean Manufacturing tools with this company, but the one I remember most was their 5-S event, because it had such an impact on Curt.

We examined what you see on the shelves at the far end of the building in the *"Before"* picture. Much of that material had been on those shelves since they had moved into the building 16 years earlier. One of the lathes you see in the foreground no longer worked and the other one was idle because it was no longer needed in their process.

During the 5-S event, the team dispositioned as scrap (recycled), over 20,000 pounds of obsolete material. They donated usable equipment and materials to the local community college and we cleared hundreds of square feet of floor space previously occupied by unused equipment and materials.

Illustration 4.2   "After" condition 5-S project

Finally, there was enough space to move Curt into the main building! Now Curt operates right next to his team mates, in a well lit, well heated environment. His life got better because of Lean. And, oh yes, they let him bring the cat!

Just a side note; the company owner, largely retired would often come in around 3:00 PM everyday just to see what was going on and to be around the shop. After all, he started the company… it was his baby.

He would sweep up or help in any way he could. He basically just wanted to be around. During our 5-S event, the team filled countless dumpsters with what they deemed to be scrap for recycling. The next day we would find some of the same parts we threw away the previous day back on the shelves. We found out that after the kaizen team would leave for the day, the owner would go dumpster diving; retrieving parts that he just couldn't bear to part with.

What to do?

The team decided to have the recycling company pick up the dumpsters at 2:30 PM every day; a half hour before the owner arrived. After all, he hadn't noticed the material on the shelf for the past 16 years; if he never saw it leave, there was little chance he would miss it in the future! By storing unneeded and obsolete material on the shelf they were losing valuable manufacturing space.

Sometimes you have to be creative!

Chapter Five

My best (worst) training experience

It was 1992 and I was new to consulting. It was the coldest part of winter and the consulting company I had joined was just wrapping up a project, in the coldest part of the nation. A ninety minute drive east of Minneapolis – St. Paul. Nothing could have prepared me for the environmental contrast between the warm rains of the Oregon Coast and the 40 degrees below zero (wind chill) of Chippewa Falls, Wisconsin in mid-February.

When I checked into the hotel the clerks told me that surrounding lakes and rivers were frozen three feet thick. Actually, they seemed proud of it; like people in the high desert of Central Oregon bragging about their 300 days of sunshine per year. It was my first trip to visit this particular client, but was probably the last of ten or twelve such visits by my consulting team over the previous year or so.

The company had about 130 employees. This was not the kind of machine shop I was used to; here they did heavy duty machining. These guys used ten foot long vertical mills and surface grinders to force huge cutting tools into blocks of steel that weighed in at 3,000 pounds. They would drive tool after tool into (what seemed to be impenetrable) high carbon steel until the final product emerged looking like a chrome plated miniature roller skate park.

By the time they were completed, these sculptured steel blocks would lose up to half their weight to the unmerciful screaming spindle of a CNC machine. The "sculptures" would then be put into use as an extrusion die for the plastics industry.

Illustration 5.1 Horizontal Mill Source: http://www.exapro.com

The parts were complex and heavy. They were very difficult to engineer, program, and run on the enormous machines. Some of the set-ups on these machines required hours to complete.

The value of this vertical milling machine while it was running (or in their words: "making chips") was over $7.50 per minute. The company had agreed that despite the application of other Lean tools, Set-Up Reduction would have to be the next step.

Looking back now, I can just imagine Dave (my boss, the president of the consulting company I worked for) taking a figurative look at the fifteen guys he had on his payroll and asking himself, "Let's see, who should we send to the coldest place on earth?" It goes without saying that Dave's attention fell on the new guy, me!

So, I showed up at a lakeside restaurant that the client had rented to train the last group of 40 machinists. Try to imagine 40 meat eating, burly, Wisconsin machinists who were used to tossing around 3,000 pound blocks of steel, all dressed in buckskin colored double-faced Carhartt dungarees, red flannel shirts, and steel toe boots. They seemed strangely out of place sitting in the upscale steak house conference room!

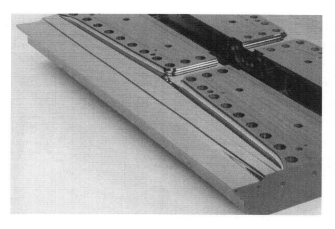

Illustration 5.2 Extrusion Die Source: http://news.thomasnet.com

In a demonstration of probably the best work ethic I have ever seen, they were already in their seats when I dragged in at 7:00 am, silently cursing the two hour time difference.

They were sitting quietly (maybe a little too quietly) around a huge U-shaped table in the cold (cold, cold) basement of what looked like the only eating establishment for miles around. As I handed out the 300 page workbooks and assembled the overhead projector, (we didn't have laptops or projectors back then) they continued to sit silently and either stare at the unopened books before them or lean back in their chairs with their size 14 boots crossed and eyes closed.

The plan was for me to train the entire team of 40 machinists during the first 2 days of the workshop and then select a machine as a target area. The team would then select a smaller group of 7-8 team members to address Set-Up Reduction for the last three days of the week. The entire team would then come back together on Friday afternoon to hear the kaizen team's presentation.

After initial introductions we got started with what would be the longest day of my training career. For the entire first day of class all I saw was the *tops of their heads*. I got *no* eye contact, I had *no* engagement, and I got *no* voluntary response to my questions! I received *no* feedback, questions, or visible interest. They were obviously resistant to training and change of any kind.

Even though I was new to consulting, I knew I was in trouble. So the next morning instead of opening up my box of slides, I just pulled up a chair and sat down beside the overhead projector. I sat there silently for a moment as they slowly stopped talking to each other and turned their focus to me, obviously wondering why I was just sitting there.

I finally said "I don't know you guys. You don't know me. I don't have time to figure out what's going on here, we only have one more day of training. And I don't have time to use trial and error to find out what the *burr under the saddle blanket* might be. I am not inclined to see your company spend money on you and me to be here for another day like we spent yesterday." They were passing nervous glances back and forth. I definitely had engagement! Now I had eye contact! "I need to find out why you are not engaged in this process, or I think that I will let your management team know that this is a waste of time and money, and I will go get on a plane back to Oregon." It was a bit of a bluff, I know. But I had to get their attention. "So, what is it?" I paused "What's the problem? Is it that I am from Oregon, is it that my background is in the sheet metal industry instead of machining? Is it the way I wear my hair? What?!"

Then I sat there beside the overhead projector for the longest 30 seconds of my life. Just stop and watch the second hand on your clock for half a minute. Imagine sitting in front of three dozen burly, bearded, snowmobile riding, beer drinking machinists whose average weight had to be over 200 pounds (and that would be without their steel toed boots); which, by the way, I was beginning to imagine striking me in the head. Anyone of them could have snapped me like one of the frozen twigs brushing against the frost covered windows.

Total silence.

Then off to my left someone finally broke the unbearable silence with the comment; "Lean manufacturing won't work here!"

"OK!" I surprised myself by how loud I responded. "Tell me about that. Why won't it work here?"

He took a look around the room as if to survey his teammates for their permission to speak. "Last month the V.P. ..." and he went into a rant about something the Vice President of

Operations had done. In his mind Lean was counter-productive to anything that the manufacturing team had been working so hard on for the past year.

Then, someone on the other side of the room chimed in. "Not only that, but last spring they...." He went on to recall a six month old management decision that required excessive effort by his team but was viewed as *unshared* by those in the administrative process.

Then it seemed like everyone was talking at once. Spewing reason after reason why Lean Manufacturing would never work at their company. I had to jump up and grab a felt pen to write down their comments on a flip chart. We filled the better part of two flip chart pages with their opinions, concerns, comments, and observations from current situations as well as examples from the previous six years or so.

My head was swimming. I told them to take a break. I thought to myself: "I need to call Dave...(my boss) ...he will know what to do."

We didn't have cell phones back then (just pagers). So I went to the payphone and called the office knowing that Dave would be able to enlighten me on the next steps I should take. He probably had twelve plus years of experience working with teams like this.

"Dave's not here..." came the frightening answer from the other end of the phone line.

What to do? I was beginning to panic!

Then a B.F.O. (blinding flash of the obvious) occurred. I don't know where it came from or what triggered it, but I suddenly recalled something I had read years earlier in Stephen Covey's book "Seven Habits of Highly Effective People." He had explained the concept of the circle of concern and circle of influence.

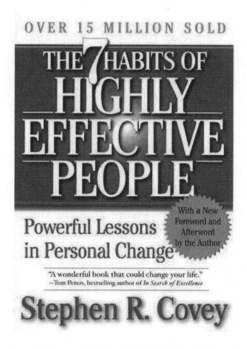

Illustration 5.3 Seven Habits of Highly Effective People cover

In a nutshell, we all have both. We would like to think that we have influence over everything. But unless we are Donald Trump, we actually have rather limited influence over the many things that we are concerned about.

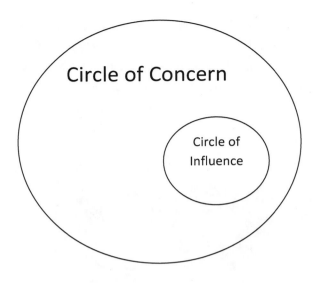

Illustration 5.4 Circle of Influence / Concern (Stephen Covey)

For example, I am concerned about world hunger, but I have limited influence over that. I could send an entire ocean liner of food to starving kids in another country, but the government of that country might intercept the shipment and trade it for weapons rather than choosing to feed their own people. I may have influence to help people in my own community, but if I spend all my time, resources, and energies trying to influence something that is obviously outside my circle of influence or control then I inhibit the chance I have to improve things which are actually within my control.

So this was the concept I needed to share with the team in Wisconsin.

I gathered them back together and explained Covey's concept and then we worked through the list of issues that they had generated as "reasons Lean Manufacturing would not work in their company."

I put a check mark beside each item that they determined was within their control and we left unchecked the items that they felt were outside their sphere of influence. Of the fifteen or so items on the list, only two or three were actually something that they viewed as within their control.

I explained that neither they nor I could hope to change those unchecked items. However, I promised them that if they worked with me for the rest of the week by focusing on the items on the list we deemed *within* their sphere of influence, I would show them how they could use their influence to make their jobs better, easier, more profitable, and more secure. They agreed, and for the remainder of the workshop I had terrific engagement and participation.

They selected and carried out a Set-Up Reduction project on a vertical mill, netting an annual savings of $96,000. Since they had three such machines in their plant, they determined that they could triple that savings number if they applied the same approach to each of the two similar machines.

So, what started out to be the worst training experience in my life became one of the most rewarding. It would not have been so if I had not been able to pull out that idea gleaned from reading Stephen Covey's book. That concept (arrow) would not have been in my arsenal (quiver) had I not taken the time to read it a few years earlier.

The message is this; "You have to fill your quiver with arrows before you go into battle."

Once you are on the battle field it's too late to think about preparing yourself. Self education is so important when you are leading teams. You never know when or from where a "Dragon" is going to appear. You need to have your *quiver* completely full and your *bow* ready.

Chapter Six

"People Depend on Me!"

My first experience with leading a team was challenging and fulfilling to say the least. At the time, I was a journeyman press brake operator in a unionized precision sheet metal shop. We made everything from go-carts for Malibu Grand-Prix to birthing beds for Adel Medical. We were also riding the high-tech wave; fabricating computer chassis for Tektronix, Sequent, and Fujitsu, printer stands for Hewlett Packard, and anything else the sales team could drag through the door.

Illustration 6.1 Archive photo

I joined the company in 1983 and worked my way through every department, even serving as Quality Assurance Manager for a period of time. Then around 1986 our largest customers started asking us to provide product on a program they called

"Just in Time". We didn't know JIT from a hot rock, but that didn't stop our sales team from promising the moon to buyers.

In the past we might have made a monthly batch size of 600 units, but now the customers were demanding 150 units per week with the goal of someday reaching an ideal pull system of 30 units per day! It didn't seem to dawn on the sales personnel that if a computer chassis has 80 complex sheet metal parts in each unit, and each part requires about a half hour to set-up on a CNC machine, then the time spent in set-up mode per order would be about 40 hours. Doing this once a month was bad enough, but doing it four times every month meant that our team was now spending 160 hours of labor performing set-ups. That meant a significant reduction in the available time we had to actually *run* parts.

Our company started hemorrhaging money. Our customers suggested that we explore what companies like Toyota were doing. In desperation we read books, we went to seminars. We even went to Japan to find out how the most forward-thinking companies were accomplishing what seemed to us an incredibly complex transformation.

It turned out that there *was* a science to it, but it was *not* rocket science. We spent the next few years focusing on the fundamentals: Set-Up Reduction, developing best practices, re-engineering the parts to make them easier to set-up, 5-S (workplace organization), cross training, and others. Things got much better, but not good enough. We soon hit a performance plateau.

The only way to break through was to completely re-design the way we did business. We had to change the way we moved parts and information. Our company president decided to take about 10% of the population (8 out of 80 people) and put us on a 3-day work week; Fridays, Saturdays, and Sundays working 12 hours a day. We were given a percentage of the workload and were permitted to try as many of the innovative tools we had been reading about and had observed during our visit to Japan.

They held a company meeting to explain the plan and identified me as the team leader. They put a sign-up sheet in the lunchroom and invited any and all personnel to sign up for the new shift. They did a good job of selling the 3-day work week shift! Not only extolling the benefits of having four days a week off, but emphasizing that the team would be left alone for the most part; autonomous, self directed, not under the thumb of a traditional management team, able to get creative, try anything and everything they wanted to try, including doing their own hiring, setting their own vacation schedules, and on-and-on.

So, guess who volunteered?

All the rebels, all the renegades, the dysfunctional, anti-social, undependable, grouchy, and isolationists in the company; that's who signed up.

When I saw the short list of candidates I realized two things:

1. I was on a sinking ship.

2. This was going to be the worst working experience of my life.

But, over the next six months or so, our team became one of the most productive teams I have ever worked with (before or after). I cannot put into words exactly what it was, but there was a creative stew assembled in that rag-tag group of individualists that somehow came together in the pressure vessel that our company president was cooking with.

Every person on my team had a unique and challenging issue to deal with. One person (let's call him Ernie) was anti-social. You could say "good morning!" and you would get absolutely no response. Marie had anger issues. Only Marie and God knew what she was so mad about. She seemed to have disdain for most men, and didn't seem to like women much either. Everyone on the other shifts encouraged her to "Go sign up for that week-end shift. That sounds like something you would really be good at!"

José was a hard worker and very dependable, but he was like a nervous chihuahua dog on crack cocaine. You couldn't get him to focus on anything for more than thirty seconds; Atomic ADHD!

Blaine was neither a great performer nor dependable. Young, but old enough to drink, he was quite the party animal. He had been assigned to my team by another supervisor who had basically told him that this was a part of his "last chance agreement". Blaine's attendance problems had been a thorn in the side of every department supervisor since he had been hired. No amount of coaching, supervising, unpaid days off, threats, or last chance agreements had ever been successful in turning Blaine's attendance problem around. So, they shoved him off on me.

We started at 6:00 AM on Friday morning. Blaine would usually show up about first break. During lunch he would retreat to his multi-colored, multi-dented, 20 year old Datsun pickup to sleep. Then he would come back into the shop and attempt to eat a cold hamburger with one hand while trying to run his machine with the other.

No one on the team could stand Blaine.

In reality, everyone on the team hated everyone else on the team.

After the first month I realized that if this group was ever going to have a chance of becoming a high-performing team, I was going to have to take positive and immediate (and maybe desperate) measures.

I decided to use a technique called the peer to peer review. I sat the team down on a Sunday afternoon, just before the end of the shift. I asked them to list the names of people (living or dead) that they would consider a "world class" person. They rattled off names like Mother Theresa, Martin Luther King, and Jesus Christ. I asked if I could add one or two, and with their permission I added Cal Ripken (a baseball player called the "iron man" who had not missed a game in 2,131 starts).

Then, beside each name I asked them to find a one-word characteristic that made the person stand out as a world class example. Beside Mother Theresa's name they had me write down "helpful", because she cared about others and always tried to help them. Beside Martin Luther King's name they selected the word "visionary" because he had "a dream" and was somehow able to implant that same vision into the minds of millions (maybe billions) of other people's minds. When we got to Cal Ripken's name, they hesitated until I reminded them

59

of the amazing record number of consecutive games he played. They decided that "dependable" was the word that best described this key characteristic.

We created a list of about 10 key characteristics that we thought were attributes that a world class team, and everyone on *our* team, would benefit from developing into strengths.

I asked them if they would be willing to give each other (myself included) feedback on how we were each doing in terms of demonstrating these 10 characteristics. I would send home a review form with each team member every Sunday for the first few months. After ten weeks or so, we began conducting those reviews monthly. We would anonymously rate each other on a scale of 1-5; five representing strength in regard to a particular characteristic, one representing a large opportunity for improvement.

Peer-to-Peer Evaluations

Characteristic	Jan	Fran	Stan	Dan	Leanne
Positive attitude					
Self motivated					
Open to new ideas					
Willing to help out					
Communicates well					
Dependable					
Organized					
Wants to win ! ! ! !					
Team Player					
Average					

Figure 6.1   Peer to Peer evaluation form (blank)

60

The process had to be well facilitated. It couldn't be a rock throwing contest, and it couldn't be a popularity or loyalty thing. It couldn't be about whether I would want to go out for a beer or spend time away from work with any particular person on the team or not.

It had to be honest, open feedback about the specific time period being surveyed. This wasn't about what happened three months ago, but just the person's performance during the last week, month, or whatever time period we were measuring.

We rated each person on each characteristic, including ourselves. I would collect and tally the anonymous responses every Friday (our first day of the week) and then I would privately share the results with each team member as time allowed throughout the week. No one saw anyone else's scores, they only saw their own scores and the team average.

Characteristic	Stan	Average
Positive attitude	2	3.0
Self motivated	1	3.0
Open to new ideas	3	3.4
Willing to help out	4	2.7
Communicates well	1	4.0
Dependable	5	3.0
Organized	4	4.0
Wants to win!	4	4.0
Team player	4	4.0
Average	3.1	3.5

Figure 6.2   Peer to Peer evaluation form (filled out)

61

Imagine what a powerful tool this was for a supervisor. It wasn't my opinion. It was the opinion of the entire team, their peers and co-workers. This tool gave me a chance to acknowledge them in areas where their teammates saw them having a particular strength, but also provided me an opportunity to ask them "Which behaviors do you feel might need to be adjusted so that your team sees this 'opportunity' (we never said 'weakness') becoming a strength?"

I am an old bow hunter, and I can tell you that if you put a target in front of me when I am shooting I will always try to hit the bull's-eye. People want to succeed. They want to be viewed as capable and competent, especially by their peers. While this peer review process didn't make any overnight changes, I slowly saw the values going up, and so did they. They watched and they saw the cause and effect of their actions in the feedback responses to and from each other.

My team and I experienced first-hand the results of expressing unfiltered frustration to teammates and having peer feedback about such show up in the peer review. They saw the nearly immediate effect of shortcutting the emotional needs of another team member reflected in the week after week review. It was as close to *real time* feedback as I could get, and they were interested in seeing the scores every time.

Within a year I saw tremendous personal growth from everyone (including myself), and I can only attribute the growth to the peer to peer feedback process. This once dysfunctional team was now a world class example of cohesion and self direction. They even ended up getting their photograph on the cover of a national trade magazine!

Out of respect for their privacy I am not including that photograph here. But it was certainly one of the proudest moments in my life to see their smiling faces splashed on that magazine cover. That photo also provided confirmation that I had selected the right tool to assist all of us in developing hidden potential within each of us. They (we) were at last a team that anyone would be proud to be a part of.

When I left the company to begin my consulting career, I sat down privately with each member of my team and videotaped an interview with each of those original teammates. I asked the same three questions of each team member.

1. What did we do right?

2. If we had a chance to do it over what should we have done differently?

3. What did you personally learn from this experience?

When I got to Blaine (our historically most undependable team member), I was surprised by his answer to the last question.

His answer to question #3 was "I learned that people depend on me. We work to takt time, everything has to keep flowing. If I come in late, it corrupts the flow of material. We will end up working late on Sunday if any one of us lets the others down."

Blaine had become one of the most dependable people on my team. No amount of coaching, supervising or bossing him around had ever worked in the past, but the peer to peer review process did have an effect.

I have since used the same process countless time and have decided that there are few other tools quite as effective as this one for helping to quickly develop a team to maturity.

You may visit our Website or email a request for a copy of the Peer to Peer (MS Excel) spreadsheet that we used (you can modify it for your use).

Chapter Seven

Drying paint in one minute

When my wife and I found out that we were going to have a baby, we decided that my consulting practice was going to have to be put on hold for a couple of years; enabling me to spend more time at home getting to know our son. I took a full time position with a secondary wood manufacturer. They supplied component parts to companies like Pella Windows, Anderson Doors, and countless other companies as well as private parties.

A customer might walk in with a broken piece of crown moulding from the 1914 Victorian Bed and Breakfast that he or she was remodeling, wishing to match it. "We've been to every lumber yard in Central Oregon" they might say "No one has this profile! It's like the original builders milled it themselves."

Chances are they did; or they may have had it made by a neighbor who just happened to have moulding equipment capable of producing millwork. To find an exact match for their remodeling project would be about as likely as running across an original Picasso!

So the company I worked for offered "short run" engineering services and custom moulding products alongside the huge orders being provided to the big box stores and OEM's (original equipment manufacturers) like Pella. The average lead time for custom moulding was about six days.

The material would first be cut from a standard size blank; a process called re-sawing, where the blank is cut into two identical tapered slabs. The material is pre-cut at an angle because most lineal moulding is tapered and the angular pre-cut saves moulding time and material.

After re-sawing, the material was stacked, banded, counted, labeled, and taken by forklift to a warehouse for storage. The average time spent in this warehouse (at the time) was two days. When the moulding team signaled that they were ready for the material, the forklift driver would locate the material, retrieve it, and deliver it to the appropriate moulding machine. Again, after moulding, the newly profiled material was stacked, banded, counted, labeled, and transported again to the warehouse where it sat for another two or three days waiting the paint crew's signal that they were scheduled to run the product. Another forklift movement was required to move the material to a temporary storage location, and then finally into the paint queue.

The paint crew would then un-band the bundle of freshly machined wood and feed the parts end to end on a continuous belt that directed the material through a small in-line paint booth.

Looking much like a miniature car wash, an electric eye would *see* the board coming, squirt a quick blast of paint, primer or sealer onto the piece and then deposit the painted moulding onto a slow moving cross transfer belt inside an 80 foot long drying oven. The natural gas fired furnaces maintained a constant 105 degrees Fahrenheit temperature. The belts moved just fast enough to cover the 80 foot oven length in about six minutes.

For the previous 35 years in business, the company had been painting wood this way. Experience had shown that if they tried to *hurry* the process by raising the temperature, speeding up the belt, or shortening the length of the drying belt, problems and defects increased.

Current State Map

Illustration 7.1 "Before" condition; wood manufacturing case study

Wood is a living, breathing thing. There are cellular structures that if overheated, can (for lack of a better word) explode! Pitch pockets break open, the sticky fluid *wicks* to the surface, making the paint impossible to dry. The result is unhappy customers paying for moulding that is stuck together in the shipping container, often breaking or splintering when effort is applied to separate them.

After painting, the parts were inspected, stacked, counted, banded or boxed, labeled for shipment, and moved for the *tenth time* by forklift.

We will come back to this story after a slight detour. When I first visited this company I was given a tour of the plant. As we walked around the 400 person facility I noticed that they had what seemed to me to be an inordinate number of forklifts. In fact I counted 18 forklifts. When the VP of Operations and I sat down after our tour I asked him if what I observed had been correct. He said "Yes, but it's worse than that. We work two, sometimes three shifts." So there are at least 36 forklift drivers.

I borrowed the calculator on his desk and quickly calculated that if a forklift driver made $12.00 per hour ($25,000 per person per year) then they were paying about $900,000 per year for moving material around their plant.

I asked the Vice President how comfortable he would be to cross the street to a fictitious company I called "Material Movers R Us" and write them a one million dollar check to take over their material moving activities. The idea seemed ludicrous. It was, of course. But they were in effect doing that, and had been doing so for the past few decades.

My job is to look at non-value added activities and make them unbearable. One of our first objectives at this company was a simple one; cut all forklift driving in half.

Back to our story.

The kaizen team designed a new manufacturing cell that could re-saw, mould, paint, dry, inspect, and package custom lineal moulding all in one motion. The throughput time went from six days down to 1 minute and 27 seconds. 1 minute of that time was to dry the paint.

You may be asking the same question their management asked: "Wait a minute, it takes six minutes to dry paint on wood. Thirty five years of experience tells us so!"

No one on our kaizen team was an engineer, or a painting expert. But we had the power of inventive minds and creative, open minded team members! We set up and experimented with different kinds of heat. Instead of forced air gas furnaces, someone came up with the idea of not heating the entire piece of wood, but just the surface of the painted area. By applying infrared heat from an *off the shelf* space heater (like you might find at an outdoor bus stop), we were able to test direct heat verses indirect heat.

The old process held the oven temperature at a constant 105 degrees for six minutes. We set up an experiment to raise the surface temperature of the wood to a blistering 160 degrees for just ten seconds, quickly cooling it down to 70 degrees with a series of fans. Then back under an IR heater for another ten seconds, back to a fan, back to another IR heater and finally a fan. We were able to dry the paint within sixty seconds and in a space of ten feet instead of eighty feet.

The entire cell fit in a space roughly twice the size that the moulder originally occupied by itself. This was a reduction of 9,000 square feet previously covering warehouse storage space, in-feed and out-feed equipment, and stack down areas. The value of manufacturing space in this area of the country averaged about $7 per square foot per year. This includes cost of leasing, maintaining, heating, and lighting the area. Freeing up 9,000 square feet means a potential $63,000 of cost had been eliminated annually.

Future State Map

Illustration 7.1 "After" condition; wood manufacturing case study

The team also eliminated 5.5 days of inventory worth $55,000. The cost of constructing the new *cell* was $40,000, so it basically cost them nothing. Plus they got to immediately put $15,000 onto the bottom line; money previously tied up in inventory.

The best part of this project for the customer is that depending on backlog, they can get their product delivered in about four hours instead of waiting six days under the previous process.

The company also saw a savings in labor cost. The old process required over eight people, the new process requires only five; an additional annual savings of $75,000.

An unexpected benefit was the speed at which they ran the product. Because of the traditional disconnect between moulding and painting. A moulder operator would generally run the material at 250 lineal feet per minute trying to maintain a quality dimension referred to in the industry as *knife marks per inch.*

If pushed faster than that, there was a risk that after painting; there could be a condition referred to as *"raised grain"*; an unacceptable *fuzzy* appearance to the wood. The moisture in the paint would raise the grain up like little hairs. This characteristic was partially dependent on the nature of the wood itself, but could not be predicted without seeing the wood being painted in *real time.* Now that the processes are tied together, the moulder operator could immediately see the result of the painted wood; permitting him (at times) to run the machine as high as 310 lineal feet per minute with no degraded product. Nearly a 25% gain in machine capacity.

At a current run rate (sales) of $10,000 per day, this increase in capacity equates to a potential of $625,000 new revenue per year.

Granted, this increase in sales is only *potential*, it is only there if their sales team can sell it. But, that is why Lean applies to everyone in the company and not just the shop. Once an improvement is made, then the sales team needs to work to develop new markets or build sales with the current customer base in order to capitalize on the gain.

Chapter Eight

"What if I train them and they leave?"

In the early 1990's I was approached by a precision sheet metal trade consortium to assist in developing a training course for their industry.

Thirty local competitors had been cannibalizing each other's workforce for years during the 1980's high tech boom. They wanted to develop a training program that focused on the unique processes and equipment in their shops.

Once the text book and curriculum were developed and approved, I asked them who they had in mind to teach the course. They responded with "We don't know yet." I raised my hand. While it meant a significant reduction in income, I wanted to try my hand at teaching college. It was one of the most enjoyable and personally satisfying experiences of my life! I still get phone calls, emails, and correspondence from former students. It is a powerful thing to realize that you have influenced someone else's life in a positive way.

But I eventually went back to working within the industry. I realized that although the college was fortunate to have machine tool manufacturers provide a few pieces of equipment, they could not possibly provide the many and varied kinds of machines, materials, part configurations, and engineered drawings that my students would be sure to see in the shops of the companies that would eventually hire them.

I realized that companies need to have an effective and efficient manner of training *inside* the walls of their own company.

There are subjects like shop math or basic blueprint reading that the community colleges and technical schools can do exceptionally well; but, when it comes to specific machine tool education, no school system can hope to provide the level of detail and variety that a company deals with, or that employees will see day to day.

On the other hand, the majority of the *on-the-job* training systems I've seen are marginal at best. Companies are not in the business of training. They are in the business of making parts, or delivering services, or both. Training is viewed as a necessary evil. It is something they begrudgingly make an effort to accomplish; but it is usually viewed as an investment, or worse yet a liability; a drain on resources rather than an activity that generates money in the short term.

Since they are not naturally good at it, most manufacturer's training systems are cobbled together out of a sense of desperation; in the process, trainees, trainers, and companies often suffer together (emotionally and financially) with the result.

I came to the conclusion that there are four important elements to an effective training system.

1. A subject matter expert

2. Trained trainers, capable of effectively transferring knowledge

3. A documented training outline and supporting curriculum

4. Available equipment, materials, and products

Community colleges have two of the four things necessary to carry out an effective training system. Most manufacturing companies have the other two.

Community colleges have trained trainers, and they are experienced at developing course materials, outlines, and curriculum.

The companies have the other to critical elements; subject matter experts and machines, along with the materials, documentation (prints, job travelers, routers, process procedures), and other details about which employees need training in order to effectively and safely operate equipment or to process material (or services).

I realized that if I could provide the companies with trained trainers, an easy to maintain curriculum, and training outline then they would have *all four* critical elements of an effective training program.

So in 1995 I published my first book: "High Involvement Training" published by Fabricators and Manufacturers Association.

Companies shy away from training for two reasons; first, they fear that a meaningful training program will require development and maintenance of a 6-inch thick binder describing the 'body of knowledge' necessary for every single process in the shop. Trying to document the knowledge gained by a journeyman machinist or sheet metal operator (or any process for that matter) over years of work experience certainly seems like a monumental task!

Second, there is often a fear that once they are trained, employees may figuratively "cross the street" to a competing firm for more money.

The general manager of one company put it very bluntly: "What if I spend all this time, effort, and money to train them and they leave?"

My partner at the time responded with another question (I wish I would have thought of it): "Yes...but what if you don't train them and they stay?"

He got the point. The risk of losing good people will always be there, but by providing them meaningful, rewarding work, effective training, and a visible pathway (roadmap) to help them visualize the steps required to make personal progress and advancement, you will probably retain the best workers anyway.

Both of these fears are unwarranted. Experience with setting up over a dozen in-house colleges has shown that an effective outline for each process can be produced in just a couple of days. Coupled with an effective curriculum (we collect samples and examples of material we need to use for training, and store them in *banker boxes*), the result is a training system that is documented, repeatable, easy to teach, easy to maintain, and requires little effort to keep up to date.

Illustration 8.1 Banker boxes containing training curriculum

Seeing a need to help companies overcome the unreasonable fear of training, I set about developing a train-the-trainer course, with the goal of helping companies do a better job of transferring knowledge from the people who had the skills to the people who needed the skills.

The first company with which I worked to set up an in-house college ended up with 42 different classes, all being taught by the subject matter experts (the operators). We had the operators attend a three day train-the-trainer class (even this class was eventually taught on-site by operators). Here they learned skills to effectively transfer knowledge. They learned to create an environment conducive to learning. They got a chance to practice utilizing effective training characteristics, develop outlines, deliver and record training, as well as administer meaningful assessments (tests) measuring the degree to which trainees had mastered and retained new skills.

The company also began rewarding people for sharing knowledge rather than hiding it. In the old days, as a machine operator I was paid more money than most because I was a highly experienced operator. When I would go on vacation, for a week at a time, there was usually a large pile of parts waiting for me upon my return. They knew that I was really good at doing those particular parts. This system made me feel very secure in my job.

It had taken me a lifetime to gain my experience and my company was rewarding me by higher pay to keep that that experience to myself.

We knew that we had to change that mind-set. We began experimenting with pay systems; trying to find a way to reward skilled operators for sharing instead of hiding knowledge. We offered our best operators a 15% bonus if they were willing and able to train others.

By mentoring less experienced operators through the use of an outline and standard practices, the effectiveness of our team more than offset the cost of the training bonus system. One company even purchased glossy business cards for their training team. With their photograph, and the title 'Master Trainer', these former black-magic practitioners were now willing and able to transfer knowledge and set-up secrets that they previously hid in countless little black books locked inside their tool boxes.

Chapter Nine

With them, not to them

On one trip to Edmonton, Alberta a manufacturer of oil pipeline equipment asked me to facilitate a 5-S (workspace organization) project. The target area was in a machining center. The operator of this horizontal boring machine was not available; he had been off work for over two months due to an accident (unrelated to work). I was a little uncomfortable going into this gentleman's area without his knowledge, so I suggested that they give him a call and let him know what we were up to.

To everyone's surprise he said that he wanted to come to work and observe. His back injury prevented him from any heavy lifting or from physically moving things around, but he did a lot of directing of where things belonged, and he was a great resource while providing a lot of open-minded assistance. This man's work area was located hundreds of feet from the tool room, and in an effort to avoid redundant trips to and from the common tool distribution area he would 'squirrel' away drills, taps, and even a $600 magnetic drill meant to be used as a shared resource with everyone else in the shop!

When we cracked open the six cabinets in his work area, we stood in awe at the collection of tools he had accumulated over the years. The value of this collection easily amounted to tens of thousands of dollars, but this operator intuitively understood that multiple trips to a shared tool room cost him time and efficiency. He was trying his best to minimize that waste.

Illustration 9.1 Before condition; Machine shop 5-S project

He was on the right track, but what he did *not* seem to understand was that by *optimizing* his own process, he was *sub-optimizing* the rest of the plant. By stashing these tools, this operator was requiring the company to purchase multiple copies of them, and he might only use them once or twice per year. He was storing them (unused) in his cabinets while someone else spent their time searching for the same exact tool; supposedly having been purchased, but in a location unknown to everyone except our operator!

It required 13 pallets to extract the unneeded tools, fixtures, and materials from the work area. This was the 'sorting' process, the first 'S' of the 5 (5-S).

Illustration 9.2 Before condition; Machine shop 5-S project

Since the regular operator was on restricted work duty because of his back injury, we had him sit and observe while another operator set-up and ran his machine for 3 days. We instructed the regular operator to place a red adhesive dot on every tool touched by the substitute operator during those 3 days. In the meantime, I worked with a different kaizen team.

At the end of the 3-day observation, the kaizen team reassembled and developed a shadow board (straighten; the second of the 5-S's). We hung every tool that the substitute machinist had utilized during the observation within easy reach of the operator.

There would now be little need for the operator to make multiple trips to the tool room, or for him to store copies of seldom used tools at his work station now; with the exception of that rare occurrence when special tools or fixtures were required to run the machine.

We also came to recognize that this area used specific drills not utilized anywhere else in the plant, so in an effort to reduce travel to the tool room we arranged and labeled each tool in a specific location. You will notice in the photographs that we arranged the tools on a slanted surface. This is done for two reasons; first, the parts are easier to identify when needed; second, when the storage surfaces remain flat (like a typical shelf) they often become *catchall* locations for materials that do not belong there. Slanting the surface makes it nearly impossible to store materials except for the ones designated or designed to be there.

At the end of the project we had removed 2 cabinets, close to 100 drills, countless fixtures, and other miscellaneous items. I suggested to the operator that he could also consider taking his roll-around toolbox home, since we had created a shadow board that contained all the tools he required. Immediately, fear showed in his eyes; the same look we might see if we tried to take away a toddler's blanket or teddy bear. I backed down right away! After all, he had been very good about being open-minded about everything we had implemented, and I needed him to be an ally instead of an enemy. Back-pedaling, I said something like, "Well, we can leave it for now."

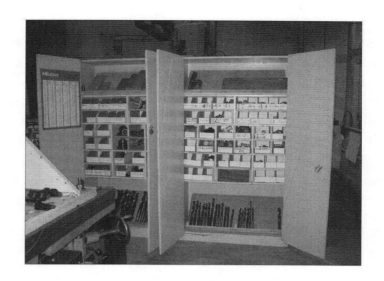

Illustration 9.3 After condition; Machine shop 5-S project

Illustration 9.4 After condition; Machine shop 5-S project

We were using his area as a model for the rest of the shop, and I wanted him to be an advocate for the change, not an unwilling participant. However, before I left for a 2-week trip back to the United States, I discretely placed a couple of strips of clear adhesive tape across the drawers of his toolbox. When I returned a few weeks later, some of the tape was still intact. With a smile, I light-heartedly pointed out what I had done. Trying my best not to be dogmatic about it, I left it at that; just planting a seed with him that he really didn't need his big roll-around tool box.

We have to effect change by doing it *with* people; not doing it *to* them. I don't know if he ever took his tool box home, but I hope at some point he will come to understand that he doesn't really need it!

For a lot of us who have worked in a shop, we can empathize with the feeling of security that having your own toolbox can provide. Some of these tool boxes become something of a status symbol. Like a pickup truck jacked up with 38" tires and oversized shock absorbers. Acquisition of these *mondo* sized roll-around toolboxes seem to become an informal completion between operators, and possibly a way to compensate for something lacking in their personal lives. I've seen toolboxes that have cost their proud owners close to $10,000, just slightly smaller than a compact car, and sometimes with better sound systems! Some of them even have onboard computers, refrigerators, and built-in microwave ovens!

We try our best to develop 5-S practices that make such grandiose toolboxes unnecessary. By applying shadow boards, *point of use* tool holding devices, elimination of threaded fastening devices, and other techniques we can often free up valuable manufacturing space by eliminating the need for many such hand tools.

Chapter Ten

Propagating tubers

In an earlier chapter we talked about the need for an effective training program. This includes teaching people how to teach. A secondary benefit to the *train-the-trainer* program is that during the three day class a group of 10-20 co-workers get a chance to see each other in an entirely different light.

Through the use of the train-the-trainer system, we have seen hopelessly dysfunctional teams draw closer; overcoming what initially seemed like impossible disharmony. One such case was at a company in Long Beach, California. The team had an equal distribution of Hispanic, Asian, Black, and Caucasian employees making up their workforce. Differences in language, cultures, beliefs, value systems, work ethics, and prejudices made my job as an outside consultant much more difficult. Trying to apply the Lean techniques among a team where the group dynamics seemed caustic at best had me considering refunding the company's check.

Before tossing in the towel, I suggested that I had seen remarkable results in similar situations by running teams through the train-the-trainer program. Now, let me reinforce the idea that this company was not yet in the process of setting up an in-house training program; they needed to adopt the Lean manufacturing system first! The train-the-trainer effort was going to be a detour and it would create a delay in the process, but I felt that any efforts to apply Lean principles without it would be temporary at best and a total waste of time at worst.

We trained two groups of 15 people over the next few weeks. The way the process works is this; the first day of training deals with how trainers need to meet the emotional needs of the learner, how to develop a training outline and so forth. The group is sent home with a homework assignment to come back the next day and teach us something that we don't know. They are free to choose any topic, but it must be unrelated to work. Preferably, they will choose a subject at which they consider themselves an expert, or at least very experienced. We have had people teach us about deep sea diving, tying fishing flies, line dancing, making salsa, rolling sushi, tuning a guitar, digital photography, and about four or five hundred other topics in this event.

Each participant is given a time limit of 10 minutes. After the presentation, the participant is given an opportunity to offer feedback to themselves; what they feel they did particularly well, or what they wish they would have done differently. Then the entire group provides feedback to that person (in the case of this company, 14 people in the audience offered each presenter feedback). The feedback must be offered in two ways; positive and corrective. The feedback must be specific, meaning that an *example* must be provided rather than just saying "That was very good". Positive feedback must include 2 statements, *what and why;* something like, "When you showed the enlarged picture of the knot, it helped me understand which direction to tie the rope." When an improvement opportunity exists the corrective feedback statement will include 2 *what* statements along with a *why* statement, like this; "Your photograph of the knot was good. Next time, you might also have a sample to hand out to each person. I think holding it in my hand would be more effective than seeing it on the screen."

I do not tell the participants the main goal of this exercise until all of the presentations are finished, but this class (when used as a team building exercise) is not really about teaching (although this is a side benefit), it is about learning how to offer and receive feedback to and from each other in a safe environment. 15 people all offering and receiving feedback 15 times means that during 2 days of participant presentations they have the opportunity to hear and offer feedback 225 times!

One of the most intriguing parts of this process for me is to watch peers come to appreciate each other in a way which they never have before. Let me relate one such experience.

One of the participants at this particular company in Long Beach was a hardcore biker. He was an imposing figure, six-foot something, a patched leather vest draped over his well worn tie-dyed tank top. A ponytail hung down the middle of his back and tattoos were on every visible skin surface. For the first half-day of class he sat virtually silent, leaning back in his chair like he was preparing for a nap. The chair to his right remained empty and he used it for an armrest. If there were other chairs available, I'm quite certain that the gentleman sitting to his left would have also found other seating accommodations.

I was not sure that our biker friend was even listening that first morning of class, so in the afternoon I pulled out all my best training techniques, including directing questions toward him without putting him on the spot...just to see if he was engaged.

He usually responded right away (although briefly), so I figured he must have been listening after all.

On day 2 we began the process of having each participant deliver their presentation. The biker walked in with an old dust-covered grocery sack, stuck it under the table at his feet and assumed a reclined position in his chair. He opted to wait through the first day of presentations, and then again until the last hour of the final day. I figured he was hoping everyone else's presentation would go *long* and he might get off without having to deliver his presentation at all! But his time did come to deliver. He halfheartedly bent down to retrieve the crumpled paper sack. He had us pass around an outline of his presentation, then he walked around to each person and deposited what looked like an old dried up potato or dirty ginger root onto the tables in front of us.

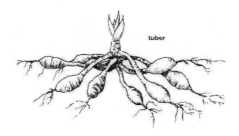

Illustration 10.1 Tuber   Source: Google images

He then took his position in front of the class and said something like this: "My presentation is; 'How to propagate tubers.'" No one dared to laugh. But, then no one knew what a tuber was either.

89

He pulled a beautiful fresh cut flower out of the paper bag. He explained how tubers are a type of bulb that becomes a flower. Iris', Lilies, Daffodils, and other such flowers are all examples of tubers.

Illustration 10.2 Daffodil   Source: thehoopers.org

There are many kinds of tubers and he told us all about them. He described how each year the flower wilts and fades away, but buried in the topsoil is a tuber (a seed) which divides and basically becomes two seeds for the next growing season. Like a dividing cell, one flower becomes two during the next growing season. Two tubers become four; four become eight, and so on.

He was running over his ten minutes, but as I looked around I realized that his co-workers were enthralled by his presentation and at the excitement and energy he had for growing tubers. Being a biker was his hobby, but growing and propagating tubers was obviously his passion. I let him go on.

This huge hulk of a man walked around the room and bent down low or kneeled down in front of each person and showed them how to *ever so gently and tenderly* separate the two interlocked bulbs. It seemed so out of place; so out of character. But for those few minutes I think he forgot himself, he lost himself in the moment of teaching. He lost himself in the dynamics of 15 people all excited and learning about something that they did not know before. The group was empathizing with his love for the amazing feat of creation and nature that they were holding in their hands. His passion was infectious and all fifteen participants were like first graders going on their first field trip to a petting zoo.

The reason we have train-the-trainer participants choose their own topic is that when the subject is something that we care about, we forget our nervousness and sharing the information and our passion about the subject becomes more important than our natural and often paralyzing fear of being asked to *present* in front of other people.

This team learned something about themselves and about each other in the process of learning how to effectively transfer knowledge. They became more respectful of each other. They had a new appreciation for each other. They had gained a new perspective (from the viewpoint of the other person). And they could now offer feedback to each other more openly, honestly, and without damaging each other emotionally. After hearing 225 examples of feedback in two days they could easily approach a co-worker and thank them for their extra effort, or even suggest an alternative to a current process (an improvement opportunity) while showing them real concern and respect at the same time.

If you have never had the experience of holding a train-the-trainer workshop in your organization, I suggest you do so sooner rather than later! You will be amazed at the improved communication, cohesion, and concern for each other that your teams will demonstrate this experience. Almost all community colleges offer some variation of a train-the-trainer program.

Chapter Eleven

Tool Room Transformed

I had just joined a large family-owned company as a fulltime continuous improvement manager. I was ninth in the organizational chart and answered directly to Bob, the President and owner of the company. He was quite possibly the most intelligent man I had ever met and rumor had it that Bob had an IQ approaching 170. He was a voracious reader and he supplied me with at least 15 of the 70 books I have in my personal library. Bob not only had a huge intellect, but he was also physically an enormous man. At 6'6" or 6'7" and easily 300 pounds, he looked like a small giant.

When I hired on for what I imagined would be a one or two year stint as CI Manager, Bob gave me the office right next to his. I think he wanted instant access to me when he had an idea or question. And he had ideas all day long, something you would expect of someone with his intellect. Our offices were on the second story of a building attached to, but separate from, the manufacturing facility. Within a couple of weeks of running up and down the stairs and trying to stay in touch with what was happening on the shop floor, I approached Bob with a concern. I expressed to him that I felt that I needed to be closer to the people doing the work.

I believe that the responsibility of anyone in the role of continuous improvement is not necessarily to be the best idea generator (not that it's a bad thing), but rather to be the best listener. Being in an office totally separated from the shop meant that I was not going to see or hear what was going on unless I went to the operators. They were definitely not going to come to me if it meant that they were going to have to track all the way through the shop, up the stairs into the beautifully carpeted floors and beautifully stained and varnished knotty pine paneled walls of the office.

So I approached Bob with an idea. I told him that I had noticed the old tool room; an unlit, dirty, old, abandoned room filled with cobwebs and the greasy remnant of a saw sharpening process that they no longer used. The tool room floor was 20 feet by 20 feet of broken and uneven concrete and the leaky roof hadn't been patched in years. Left alone for a few more years, I'm sure that stalactites would have been growing from floor to ceiling in that room! The Bulbless ceiling lights hung like antiques in a memorabilia store so the only illumination was provided by outside light streaming through holes in the un-insulated, corrugated metal walls; the result of saw blades and planer knives thrown against them by machines or possibly by frustrated operators.

So, I told Bob that I wanted to move my office to the old tool room. Bob asked me, "What do you want with that dirty old tool room?" I expressed my concern about being available and approachable to the manufacturing team. I told him that if we were ever going to be world class (his vision) we were going to have to develop 400 people into business thinkers. That was going to require daily, even hourly (real time) kaizen events. I asked his permission, but I think he knew that it was not really a request, but more of a condition of my continued employment.

It took a couple of weeks, but we completely transformed the room. I wanted it to be lit up like a doctors office, not only providing a place for kaizen teams to work, but also a place where people could come in and sit down in a comfortable old couch and eat their lunch and just talk. Part psychologist office, part kaizen war room, I wanted swinging doors that were open all the time. Instead of sheet rock for walls, I wanted the entire room to be covered in *white board*, so people could come in and never have to look for a place to write down or develop an idea. The local hardware store sold 4x8 sheets of *Shower Board* which is basically the same material as a white board.

The tool room (now kaizen room) happened to be right on the way to the main lunchroom, so it didn't take long for people to begin stopping on their way to or from eating their lunch to drop off an idea or to just stick their head in the door and grouse about some problem they were having. Soon people were coming in to eat their lunch, staying after work, and even coming in early for a cup of coffee in the morning (I brought in doughnuts from time to time to bait the *idea trap*). I made a lot of good friends at that company in the few years I worked with that team, and we made some good progress together, taking a $28million inventory to less than $7million, reducing lead time for some products by more than 90%, and improving cost, delivery, and quality in what had been a struggling business.

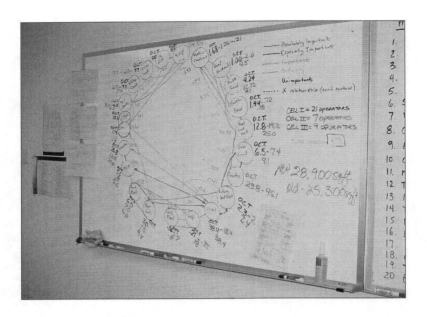

Illustration 11.1 Kaizen "war room"

My message is that while I feel completely comfortable applying the tools of Lean manufacturing and the other world class techniques, I cannot hope to be good enough to do it on my own. I need the ideas and the observations of the subject matter experts. These experts are the ones who struggle with the problems every day and they need a *real time* vehicle to communicate their problems. Without it, the opportunity to reduce or eliminate non-value added activities and the frustration associated with dealing with them daily is quickly lost in the fire-fight of the next *problem de-jour*.

You cannot effectively run a kaizen promotion office from a palace office or ivory tower. You have to get down where the action is, where you can get your hands dirty.

Chapter Twelve

The five minute MBA

As the eldest son of a bridge builder, third child in a family of eight kids, I took it as my personal responsibility to help the family after my dad was seriously injured in a bridge collapse in 1958. I was three years old when it happened. Working the night shift, Dad and his co-workers were eating their lunch while sitting on a stack of wood forms and pilings. The concrete (evidently not completely cured) broke away from their "seat" and sent a number of them falling into the river below. One man died in that accident and Dad broke his neck by falling into Oregon's Rogue River.

Obviously medical technology in 1958 did not have the same capability for repairing broken necks and spinal cord injuries as they do today. Dad was unable to work for a number of years, and the injury really never got much better as he aged. As the years went by our family struggled financially. In those days they didn't have the kind of accident insurance or welfare assistance available now, so thirteen years later at the age of 16 I quit high school to work in the North Santiam Canyon lumber mills of Oregon; viewing it as my obligation to help out the family.

The reason for the preface to this story is that I want my readers to understand that I was not in a position to attend college or obtain a degree in business management. Years later the owner of a business I worked for did me the biggest favor of my working life...he taught me to think like a business person. I

97

have since been able to work with many companies by assisting them in making decisions that have, in many cases, helped them survive and thrive as businesses.

So how did this high school drop-out become capable of assisting others (even those with multiple college degrees) in managing their businesses? Let me finish the story. In 1982 I was also seriously injured. Knocked off a log haul conveyor in the lumber mill, I broke my jaw, nearly broke my neck, fouled up my hip, and sustained a number of other injuries that haunt me to this day. As I lay in the hospital bed with my mouth wired shut, drifting in and out of pain killer and muscle relaxer-induced sleep, I reassessed my choice of careers.

I was determined to go back and finish high school, take some classes to learn to weld, read blueprints, perform shop math, and educate myself to be a machinist. As it turns out, I chose correctly! It was just at the beginning of the *high tech* economic expansion. Silicon Valley was humming and customers were begging precision sheet metal manufacturers to make their products for them. I took a job with a local precision sheet metal manufacturer, and for the next 3 years I learned the trade. I become a journeyman in the local sheet metal worker's union.

As described briefly in other stories in this book, our company was *strongly encouraged* to begin delivering to customers using a new process they called JIT (Just in Time). The encouragement came in the form of letters that included statements like: "If you are unable to deliver small lot sizes on demand, your services will no longer be required. We will begin looking elsewhere for vendors capable of providing materials 'just in time'".

After 3 years of struggling (and hemorrhaging), trying to adopt the processes applied by Toyota and others meant breaking trail. Since OEM (original equipment manufacturing) processes like those you might see at *'Toyota-like'* shops did not fit our 'Job shop' model, we found (as many companies have since discovered) that not every tool applied at Toyota is applicable in their unique environment. We finally did begin to adapt and adopt the tools that made sense, and the 100 people or so in our company all became JIT thinkers. One of the fundamental tools we began with was SMED (Single Minute Exchange of Dies), more commonly known as set-up reduction.

Early on in our transformation I was surprised when my boss initially shot me down when I approached him with an idea. He was a very forward-thinking, open-minded person and it confounded me when my idea for improvement was met with such lukewarm response. His initial pushback didn't last long, and the follow-up conversation led to a personal breakthrough that changed my working life forever. This exchange between manager (my boss) and employee (me) was such a powerful experience; a singular moment for me, that it changed my entire career. I doubt that he would even remember the exchange; he certainly cannot know what a long-lasting effect his coaching had on my life.

The lesson to be learned here is that you never know the effect you may have on a peer, employee, or even your manager when you share knowledge that they need. Teaching them to think like a business person, sharing the experience you have gained is a great gift. Obviously not everyone will take advantage of the gift, but as I relate this story take a look back in your life to see if you have taken advantage of the 'teachable moments' like my boss did with me, when they were presented to you.

In the late 1980's all of our customers wanted the parts we manufactured for them to be letter stamped...partly because of ISO 9000, and partly for internal part traceability. The machine I worked on was called a turret punch. Like the turret on an armored tank, this machine could turn 360 degrees to select any one of 50 different tools. Some tools were used to punch holes and other tools were used to impress shapes or to form the metal. One of the tools was a 3" diameter label stamp tool. The machine would index the tool under the striker and then a huge flywheel and clutch system would apply up to 30 tons of pressure in a split second. When the machine was running at full speed it really did sound like a machine gun!

The label-making tool had to include the initials of our company, a part number, the date of manufacture and current revision level. The entire label would look something like this:

XYZ 1-12-1988

ABC-3344 Rev B

Up to 30 letters and numbers needed to be changed every time we set-up to run a different part. Without counting *engineered to order* parts, we probably had over 5,000 active (repetitive) part numbers to run in our order file. With the increasingly smaller lot sizes being ordered, I probably changed this letter stamp tool a dozen times per day.

The process of changing the letter stamp tool meant that I had to remove (punch out) two, 3" long pins that held all the letters and numbers in place. Then I would remove the individual letters and numbers from the last part ran and replace them with the letters and numbers for the next part. I would then reinstall the two pins to capture and hold the letters in place (upside down and backward). Next I would measure the length of the tool and adjust it for the thickness of the new material to be processed. I would load up a sheet of sample material, test stroke the letter stamp and then examine the freshly embossed material; checking for number accuracy, part deformation, and any other defects. Then I would lock everything down or adjust the tool as necessary.

This entire process of changing the letter stamp tool required about ten minutes of time. There were six other turret punch operators doing the same thing I was doing. So, one day I had what I thought was a brilliant idea. I went to my boss and said; "Hey, if you buy me a second letter stamp tool, I could be setting it up for the next order while the machine is running the current order, and that would save me about ten minutes of machine downtime for every change!" My boss asked me how much the additional letter stamp would cost. "About $650", I replied

"Well," he paused "If I buy you one, the other operators are going to want one for their machines too." He grabbed his calculator "That's $4,500!" He looked at me over his reading glasses and said, "I can't do that!" I walked away dejected.

A few days later I spotted my boss walking toward my machine. He walked up to me as my machine was flailing away against sheet metal. He had his calculator in his hand. We made small talk for a couple of seconds, and then he got a serious look on his face. "Tell me again about that letter stamp tool." Then without waiting for a response he continued, "How long did you say it takes you to set that up?"

"About ten minutes", I replied. "And you do that about 10-12 times a day?" he questioned.

"Yeah, some times more." I could see his interest was growing.

"And you are not the only guy doing this." He looked around at the other machines running.

"Right." I could see the wheels turning in his head.

He raised the calculator and started entering in numbers, talking out loud as he stroked the keys. "10 minutes per set-up, 10 times per day, 7 machines..." He looked up at me and added "And...we work three shifts...that's 2100 minutes per day spent setting up letter stamp tools!"

"Divided by 60, that means we are spending 35 hours every day setting these tools up. What you are saying is that these $250,000 machines are down 175 hours per week." He paused. "Did you know that we charge $65.00 per hour for each of these machines when they are running? That means we are leaving $11,000 on the table every week. We have been considering buying another machine but we have almost 9000 hours of capacity on these machines per year if we just eliminate the set-up time on these letter stamp tools!"

It was impossible for me to hide my smile of satisfaction. He continued "Seven additional letter stamp tools will cost $4,500. We can pay for those in less than one week."

In five minutes he taught me to think like a business person. He did not *have* to share that thought process with me. He could have done that in his office, made the decision and bought the tools without including me in the conversation at all. But by taking the time to help me understand how to use costs to justify my idea, he provided me a great gift.

I can tell you that I never approached my boss with another idea without being able to show him the costs of not adopting it. Being an idea generator, I used that tool many times, coming to the realization that not all my ideas were *money making ideas*. Being able to calculate the benefits of an idea and measure that value against the cost sometimes convinced me to discard an idea before even approaching my boss.

My boss took his responsibility to teach the rest of us *seriously*. He *had* been fortunate enough to get his MBA, and he shared with us enough knowledge so that we were able to assist him in building a viable and sustainable business. There was also the time he came in on Sunday (the last day of my team's 3-day work week) to share a pizza lunch with us. He brought two rolls of pennies with him (one dollar).

As we all stood up to go back to work, he asked us to sit back down. He dropped the hundred pennies onto the table, saying "Last year we sold $10 million dollars worth of stuff."

I thought to myself, "He is a very rich man."

He looked around the table and added "Now, that doesn't mean I got to take home $10 million dollars." He pointed to the pile of pennies. "Pull out forty cents into a pile over there."

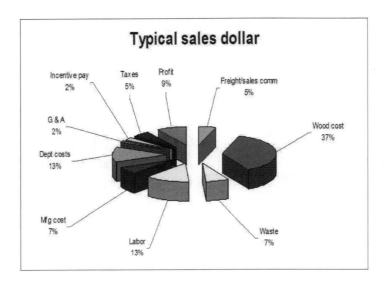

Illustration 12.1   Typical sales dollar breakdown

A couple of us counted out forty cents.

"That represents the material cost for every dollar of sales we had last year. Now scrape off seventeen cents into a pile." We did, "That's the cost of labor; what we pay to cover all your wages...for every dollar of sales we have."

Then he had us scrap together piles representing the cost of power, the cost of the facility, the cost of leasing machines, the cost of consumable items like sandpaper, sales commissions, taxes and so forth. What was left in the middle of the table was 4 pennies.

"That is my net profit from every dollar we sell." He didn't have to share this information with us but he continued, "So on

$10,000,000 in sales I get to take home about $400,000 in profit. That is, unless I want to buy some new piece of equipment or reinvest the money back into the company in some way."

"I would like there to be six or eight cents left in the middle. What can I do?" He paused to let us respond.

"Sell twice as much?" Someone chimed in.

"OK", he patiently responded "But then I'd have to hire twice as many people, buy twice as much material, build twice as many buildings, and lease twice as many machines…the profit margin ends up the same 4%."

He let us think about it for a moment. We all stared at the four pennies sitting lonely in the middle of the table.

He let us off the hook, "What if we were able to save one penny in material cost." He reached over and slid a penny back to the middle from the pile of 40 we had put together representing material cost. "And what if we were able to move half a penny from labor, and half a penny from consumable cost back to the middle of the profit pile?"

He continued until he had moved 4 pennies back to the center of the table (from all the *cost* piles), explaining that in doing so "it would have the same effect as doubling the size of the business."

It took a total of about 5 minutes for his discussion with us. But in doing so he continued to teach us to think like business owners. He helped us to realize the decisions we made in the shop every day had an enormous effect on the bottom line. The *cause and effect* principle became of utmost importance to us. He helped us to begin charting and tracking our labor costs, material costs, tooling costs among others. We were contributing members of the company not just from a front line worker standpoint, but from a business thinker's standpoint. Everyone on my team knew and felt that without their contribution the company would be less viable. While none of our names were on the sign out front, to a degree, we all felt like enfranchised owners.

If you are a manager; if you have been trained to read a profit and loss statement; if you have an MBA, then you have an obligation to share that knowledge with the rest of the people on your team. The 8th form of waste is "underutilization of people's talent". People cannot contribute fully unless they are provided the tools to do so. My boss provided me and my team an MBA; five minutes at a time. It is not rocket science, but it is a science. If *this* high school drop-out can *get it* I know everyone in your organization can as well.

Chapter Thirteen

Turning it down

Not every story can be up-beat or end positively. This one could probably be taken a number of ways. One of the shortest stories in the book, but in my mind has one of the most important messages; stay true to yourself and your vision.

I am writing a novel, a science fiction story about nano-technology. Funny, because I am not really a science fiction buff, but am fascinated with the idea that scientists can now make machines so small that they have to be manufactured in the scale of atoms. A nano-meter is our smallest unit of measurement. Just to put it in terms we can all understand; a dollar bill is 100,000 nano-meters thick. Human hair grows at the rate of about 1 nano-meter per second.

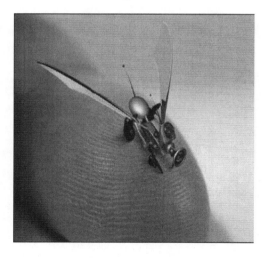

Illustration 13.1 Nanotech fly   Source scienceblogs.com

The idea that they can invent and manufacture a machine so small that it could be placed *into* the human body and directed to destroy a cancer cell or blood clot is incredible to me. So about three years ago, this idea popped into my head one night and now I am working on a story that has grown into a 250 page book.

You can imagine my excitement when a nano-technology company called last year asking about consulting services to help them become Lean! I nearly fell off my chair. I didn't tell them this, but I would probably have done the project for free, just to get the experience. We talked on the phone for quite a while; I asked about their on time delivery performance, demand patterns, number of process steps, and quality related issues.

When I asked about their waste rates (understanding that the microscopic nature of the work generally results in unusually high scrap rates), they indicated that they had a net success rate of 6%. I thought that they had misunderstood my question, so I rephrased it. "So, you mean you have a 6% scrap rate?"

"No," came the response "We only net 6%; we have a 94% scrap rate."

I almost fell off my chair again. I paused for what must have been an uncomfortable period of time for the person on the other end of the line, because they said "Hello?" evidently not sure if they had lost me.

"I'm here." It took me a second to process this information. "Well let me say, that I am very excited about the potential of working with you. But, it sounds like what you need is *not* a

Lean Manufacturing project, but rather a Six Sigma project to help identify process variability. I'm sure that we can significantly improve that rate of success."

"No," came the surprising response to my statement. "We are happy with our quality; we just need to increase our output."

I paused again, struggling to get my mind around this response.

"So have you applied any of the Six Sigma tools, like quality mapping?" I asked.

"We have been down the TQM (total quality management) road, we have process control measures in place, and we have tried some of the SPC tools." The response continued in a terse tone, "Like I said; we just need to make product faster."

Trying not to sound arrogant or condescending, I asked a qualifying question; "So you want me to help you make scrap faster?"

My efforts to avoid sounding arrogant didn't land.

"Well, if you put it like that…!" I knew the phone call was coming to an end. "We have already tried to improve our quality and that's not getting us where we need to go. We are willing to accept our scrap rate; we simply have too many orders to fill and we need help speeding up our processes."

I paused, trying to rationalize in my own mind how I could possibly turn down the best opportunity of my life to learn about nano-technology. I took a deep breath and said: "Well, I can't feel good about helping you make scrap faster, so when you are ready to take a look at Six Sigma I am here to help. In the meantime I am going to have to pass on providing you a proposal for a Lean project."

They never called back. I may have missed an opportunity to learn about nano-technology, but I am equally sure that they missed an opportunity to reduce costs and improve quality. Just imagine; if they were able to move the net yield from 6% to 12% it would have had the same effect as doubling the size of their business without the costs associated with multiplying headcount, equipment, space, and materials.

I won't kid you, it was hard to turn down this potentially lucrative project. I try my best not to be dogmatic or prescriptive when addressing the needs of the client. The customer is always right, but in this case I felt that I had to stay true to my principles.

Sometimes the patient 'doesn't know what they don't know.'

Chapter Fourteen

Sometimes I feel like Johnny Appleseed

One of the most interesting clients I have ever worked with was a small division of a Northwest Lumber Company near the Oregon Coast. When the entire crew showed up (about 200 people), the population of the little town where this company was located doubled.

I was engaged to simply show them the kaizen methodology, and they really didn't have a project picked out. The managers words were something to the effect of: "We just want you to plant the seeds; the new ideas. We hope the ideas take root and grow, but we are not unrealistic. We know that in our industry, change is hard."

We walked through the plant beginning at the log deck where they unloaded and sorted freshly cut logs. Mud-covered log trucks were constantly delivering uniform lengths of bark-covered timber about every fifteen minutes. They would unload the trucks, sort the logs by species, quality, and size and then store them until the mill requested that type of log.

The mill would determine what diameter log was needed to yield the daily cutting requirements, then the log yard would load the logs onto a special truck for the transfer to the mill. Logs were slabbed, ripped, and cross-cut into recognizable dimensional lumber. Then they were automatically stacked and transferred by truck, *green* (not dried) to an on-site planning mill. Here, screaming planers consumed the rough-sawn lumber

111

at one end and spewed out shiny finished boards from the other end.

Again, the wood was sorted by grade and length, then neatly stacked, banded, and labeled, before being picked up by a forklift and moved to a huge paved (multi-acre) storage deck.

The last step in the process was to wait for a railcar or truck sales order. When an order was received, it was generally a mixed load of different grades, lengths, species, and weights. A forklift driver had to plan the best and safest way to load for the long trip from Oregon to Texas or some other destination. Then he would spend the next half hour searching and shuffling the required stacks of wood among the thousands littering the lumber yard.

Despite the enormous technological improvements made in the 30 years since I had pulled green chain as a teenager, I saw non-value added activities (and money being wasted) everywhere I looked. You could have picked a project simply by throwing a rock and selecting a target area by where the rock fell. But, I was an invited guest. The company said that the temperament of the log sorting crew, the mill, and planer crews did not seem conducive or open to new ideas. "After all," they said "this business is old school. Things change every twenty years or so in this industry rather than every few months like other segments of the economy. We are not used to change, and we don't like it." Strange words coming from a management team, but they definitely knew their workforce.

Illustration 14.1   Lumber yard

We decided that the quickest way to show an improvement while avoiding the likely conflicts among other teams would be to do a project in an area where the fewest number of people would be involved. This ended up being in the railcar loading area.

I proposed a five day project, spread over three visits. The process was not highly technical or complex and it required only one day to value stream map the railcar loading process. A second day was used to brainstorm ideas for improvement. Our initial studies, which included outfitting the forklift with a handheld GPS (Global Positioning System), showed that the average distance traveled each time a forklift loaded a railcar was 4.12 miles.

Illustration 14.2   Arial photograph of lumber yard

By realigning the storage area to more closely match the location with demand patterns (the most popular items closest to the railcar loading area), we were able to reduce the distance traveled to less than 2.7 miles; a 37% reduction. We not only saved over 4600 miles of forklift driving per year, but also 1125 gallons of diesel fuel per year; significantly reducing their carbon footprint! Not a small thing in the face of growing opposition to wood harvesting. More sustainable manufacturing practices in their industry goes far to bridge the chasm between the mill workers and the environmental interests all around them.

I never got to go back and see how they are doing. Sometimes I feel like Johnny Appleseed, leaving behind the seeds but seldom able to go back and confirm that the tree is actually bearing fruit.

Illustration 14.3   Arial photograph of lumber yard overlaid with alternative layout

My work there was to try to plant seeds of *new thought* with them, in the hopes of seeing the rest of the team incubate and grow into a flourishing Lean enterprise. I wish I could relate a story that told how they continued on the path, but I simply don't know. As always, I was an invited guest, and was not re-engaged for future work. I have often thought about them and wondered if they made continued progress; I frequently wonder if the seeds *took root*. But that's the risk of being a consultant, sometimes you plant the seeds and then you are never around to see the growth.

For their sake I certainly hope the growth has continued!

Chapter Fifteen

I do my best work in the hot-tub

When they first brought kaizen (continuous improvement) to America from Japan, they used to call the process "5 days and 1 night." That's because facilitators typically started early and worked the kaizen team late into the night. Add to that the fact that once your mind gets into the creative mode you can't sleep even when they do release the kaizen team for a few precious hours of rest! The end results were that you slept the equivalent of one night during the typical five day event.

We learned the hard way that regardless of how satisfying it is to be a part of a successful kaizen project, after experiencing the marathon sessions familiar to most early teams, few people looked forward to being selected to participate a second time. We stopped running 14-16 hour kaizen days and we quit abusing our team members. Instead, we focused on doing a better job of scoping out a project that could be accomplished without burning out our most precious resource!

Something else I learned about *learning* and *mental awareness* was from watching the PBS show Scientific Frontiers (hosted by one of my favorite actors; Alan Alda). One of their episodes focused on a study of memory and the effects of Alzheimer's, accidents, and other factors on brain function. A major contributor to brain function (or lack thereof) is stress. We are hardwired to react almost without conscious thought when faced with stressful situations. The *fight or flight* response is an example.

Having worked with hundreds of kaizen teams over the years I have come to appreciate that individuals and teams also have an interesting response to stress when it comes to being put under pressure to generate ideas. Sometimes limited amounts of stress can actually be a very productive catalyst for breaking loose the log jam of ideas stuck in people's heads. Other times, the pressure creates a vapor lock. It is often up to me as a facilitator to determine when enough pressure has been applied.

Illustration 15.1 Hot tub   Source: Google Images

In my own case, I always tell my clients that I do my best work in the hot tub. Granted, I can never get anyone to pay me for that work, but that is when I seem to be the most creative! Sitting back and looking up at the stars, completely relaxed and void of all pressures of the day I will almost always have a B.F.O. (blinding flash of the obvious).

Knowing this about myself; I have always made a point to try to make the kaizen projects fun, adding in a warm up exercise, team building exercise, or a contest of some kind. For example, one recent client team and I were laying out a new assembly area. We videotaped the *before* and *after* condition. During our initial study of the before condition, we had documented nearly 2000 feet of distance travel by the operator. Prior to viewing the *after* condition, I asked for everyone's opinion as to how far they thought the operator traveled during the improved condition. I recorded each person's guess. After I had everyone's prediction, I stood up and taped a $20 bill to the white board where we were projecting the video. I suggested that the team member, who guessed closest to the actual *distance traveled*, would get the $20.

Twenty dollars is not a lot of money, but it created as much excitement as if it had been a thousand. More than anything, I think it was just the idea of having bragging rights. The team just *lit up*, and it made the project that much more fun. In addition to improvements in the distance traveled, this team recognized a 30% reduction in assembly labor (a savings of 10's of thousands of dollars).

When people are having fun they are more creative, more productive, and in a better mood. It fosters team building, as well as a shared positive experience; the fruit of which can often be seen (and felt) months and years later. Kaizen is hard work, don't get me wrong. It's not all fun and games. But there's no reason to brutalize your teams to get results. Make it more like creative play and you will get more work done!

Chapter Sixteen

"Leave the book"

In nearly all the stories in this book I have changed the names of the characters to protect their privacy. This is the one exception to that rule. I think that this story is so powerful, so personally important to me, that out of respect for the main subject I cannot in good conscience *mask* the names.

One of the most interesting personalities I've come across was the owner of a little mom and pop machine shop in Sparks Nevada. My first introduction to Jay was in the fall of 2002. My book 'Lean Manufacturing for the Small Shop' had just been awarded the Shingo Prize. I was ecstatic. The Shingo Prize is named after Shigeo Shingo, one of the key engineers who assisted Toyota during their incredible transformation during the 1970's and 1980's. Every year the Shingo Prize committee recognizes a small number of companies, authors or contributors whom they feel positively influenced the *body of knowledge* related to world class business principles.

So understandably I was excited to give Jay a copy of my book during our first meeting. I had even purchased a special pen in expectation of signing the book for him.

My good friend Bob had coordinated the meeting with Jay. He and Jay had known each other for years. I met Bob at his office and he drove us across town to Jay's brand new building. As we pulled into the driveway, I reached inside my bag and retrieved a copy of my newly recognized book; trying hard to not look *too* proud.

Bob pulled into a visitor parking spot and turned the key off. He just sat there for a second. I waited for his queue to get out of the car. He just continued to sit there in silence. Then finally he said "Why don't you leave the book here for now."

The shock on my face had to be apparent. Probably about the same look my son gets when he finds out that the snow day his school had in January means an extra day of school in June.

I didn't know how to respond, except to trust Bob's judgment. I left the book on the car seat and we went in to meet Jay.

It was a great first visit, and we ended up doing a number of projects with Jay and his team over the next two years.

Then about 2005 Bob and Jay planned to host a public Lean Leader workshop (a five day workshop that we teach 4 or 5 times each year). A few local companies participated, along with manufacturers from all over the United States and Canada.

During the first day of training we were planning on having Jay introduce himself and his team. I was anxious to get the workshop started, but Jay just kept going. We were a half hour into the workshop when Jay dimmed the lights and queued up a video tape.

I kept looking at my watch hoping he would get the message that he was taking more time than I had expected.

The video tape was a copy of a program from the PBS program 'Profiles in Courage' hosted by actor Danny Glover.

I thought "Where is he going with this?"

The video started out with Glover's deeply intense voice: "Imagine you are the owner of a multi-million dollar company…with a secret…a secret that you can't even share with your own children."

It took a few seconds to realize that the person being profiled; the person with the secret was Jay.

Illustration 16.1 Jay Thessiens   Source: LIFE Publications

The twenty minute video described how Jay had been chastised and demeaned by a grade school teacher. How he had developed an emotional learning disorder that made it impossible for him to read.

Despite his limited reading ability, he and his wife Bonnie had taken a couple hundred dollars and turned it into a multi-million dollar business.

Although unable to read a restaurant menu or business contract, Jay relied on the partnership he had with Bonnie to manage their lives, raise three kids together, all while growing their business.

There were about fifteen workshop participants sitting in the darkened room as the video played. Jay sat in a chair at the front of the room, unable to watch certain parts of the video; like where it described his son, who had recently died in an automobile accident. It was twenty minutes of the most emotional video I had ever been exposed to. Shortly after his son's death, Jay had been approached by his church to serve as Bishop; along with two assistants, he would provide leadership of about 600 in his "ward". As part of his responsibility, he would eventually share in teaching scripture to twelve year old boys in his congregation. He realized that if he was to going to effectively carry out his duties, which included reading and responding to organizational communication, he was going to have to learn to read himself.

Jay asked a first grade teacher to privately tutor him. Her words on the video described Jay's approach to learning "I've never seen anyone work any harder than Jay!"

Imagine trying to learn to read for the first time at 58 years of age.

At the end of the video, there wasn't a dry eye in the room when they showed Jay reading a Doctor Seuss story to his grandkids, and talking about the effect this newfound ability had had on his family and in his own life.

Jay and his wife Bonnie are two of the most unassuming, humble people I have ever met. You can tell that he doesn't like to be the center of attention, especially about a topic that most people might view as a weakness. But I think he realizes that his story can be (and has been) an inspiration to others.

As I wrote this book, I happened to find myself in the Reno area, and invited Jay and his wife out for lunch; describing this book, and asking their permission to include their amazing story within this text. There are some very nice, upscale restaurants in some of the Reno resorts, and I was buying, so I figured we would go out for a fancy lunch. Jay was driving, so I was a bit surprised when he turned into Wendy's hamburger store. He and Bonnie shared an order of fries and gave me a tentative "go ahead" on the book, reserving the right to review the story for accuracy.

As I told them about my goal of providing a compilation of stories that infuse others with energy and encouragement I shared a couple of examples. I could see the emotion well up in Jay's eyes as my stories reminded him of one of his own. A long time employee had been diagnosed with terminal cancer. He was a key member of their Quality Assurance team, but due to his illness was now confined to home for the most part.

Jay and Bonnie continued to pay this man's wages for months, taking care of him and his family right up until his passing. What I found amazing was that they didn't just cut a check to make this man financially whole, but they helped him to retain his self worth and self respect by sending proto-types and manufactured parts to his home. This permitted him to utilize his years of experience and for the company to capitalize on the knowledge and critical eye of someone familiar with the organization's quality system and customer expectations. I can imagine how powerfully sustaining that was to his self esteem.

That's the kind of person and company I want to work with. I can tell you that Bonnie is a shrewd and frugal business person. I have never gotten the impression that she is a person given to *free and loose* spending of money (eating at Wendy's as an example). Yet she obviously shares Jay's passion for making personal and financial sacrifices when there is a chance to improve the lives of others who are struggling.

The *Profiles in Courage* video was obviously meant to tell Jay's story and the courage he showed. But the love, devotion and talent of Bonnie comes through as well. They are certainly a powerful team, and as Jay mentions in the video, "Where she (Bonnie) is weak, I am strong, and where I am weak, she is strong."

Together they have overcome tremendous obstacles, and in the process showed the rest of us what is possible when love, respect, and devotion are woven into a marriage and a business.

The video described the fact that over 42 million Americans are functionally illiterate. Jay has been a source of encouragement for many who suffer with this problem.

No one but Jay can know for sure; whether his incredible efforts are his way of honoring his son; whether it is his way to demonstrate evidence of his faith by taking action; or maybe for some deeply personal reason. He has overcome countless obstacles to share his story with others (including me and my class).

Since that workshop I have had a chance to spend a lot of time with Jay and his team. And I did eventually have a chance to give Jay a copy of my book.

I know that the consulting work I've participated in with Jay's team has likely saved tens (if not hundreds) of thousands of dollars; retaining and increasing sales, improving customer response times and quality of working life for Jay's employees, but I will always feel that I have gained much more than I have given through the privilege of meeting Jay, Bonnie and their family.

With Jay's permission, I often show his video to workshop participants. The lesson I try to communicate to my students is that we spend the majority of our day with our co-workers. We may think we know the people we work with.

The truth is; we may *not really* know the people we work with at all. If we take time to ask (and listen) we might just find out that their life stories are awe inspiring.

Chapter Seventeen

What I learned from Hurricane Katrina

Not all stories have a happy ending, but when life's bumps in the road teach us something I think they are worth retelling.

I was in New Orleans thirty six hours before Hurricane Katrina hit the gulf coast. I had been engaged by a furniture manufacturer. They were supplying the dressers, vanities and armoires for a local casino resort. The hotel would be twenty stories tall, and there would be twenty rooms on each floor. Small in comparison to the mega-sized Las Vegas destinations, but for this fifty person wood shop it would keep them busy for months. In fact, it was so much work that they were not quite sure how they were going to meet the extremely demanding construction schedule.

There was a better than average chance that this company had over estimated the amount of work involved, and underestimated their ability to deliver on promises made. I sensed that I had been called as an act of desperation. The owner lived on the North Shore of Lake Pontchatrain, and everyday he made his thirty mile commute across the lake on one of the world's longest bridges, plenty of time to think about the position he had put himself and his company in.

By the time I showed up (about two months before the hurricane) they had already started the hotel furniture project. Twenty hotel floors, times twenty rooms meant they needed to produce 400 bedroom sets. Using the rational of the past they started by making the biggest and most complex parts first. On my initial tour of the plant we weaved in and out of finished Armories stacked to the ceiling. I asked if this represented all four hundred. He said that it was about half of them. The balance were still being painted and assembled. They were going to try to find an inexpensive storage location to move and house the finished product until the time came for installation.

The owner was agonizing over how they were going to get all the other mating materials produced in time for the looming installation *drop dead* date. In addition to the furniture, there were mouldings, headboards, windows and doors to produce.

After the tour we sat down and talked about the construction schedule.

I asked "Is the plan to install all the armoires at once?"

"No" came the answer "They are starting on the first floor and moving up one floor per week. The sheetrock will be done on the first floor, and then following week the painting crews come in behind them as the sheetrock team moves to the second floor. After the entire floor is painted, we will have our furniture installed the following week. There are huge financial penalties for any crew who cannot keep up with the schedule. After us, the finishing crew comes in with light fixtures, mirrors, door knobs and so forth. Nobody wants to be the reason that the casino doesn't open on time. And no one wants to be penalized; the margins are not all that attractive as it is."

"So if they don't need all 400 armoires at once, why did you decide to produce them all at once?" I asked

"It is just more cost effective to produce them in as large a batch size as possible." Then sheepishly added; "Isn't it?"

"Well let's talk about that later" I grabbed a calculator. "Twenty floors in twenty weeks. Twenty rooms per week; that's five rooms per day. That's five armoires, five vanities, five dressers, five headboards, five sets of moulding every day. Is that right?

"Yes, but…" His brain was overloading "if you build a daily batch size then you will have to set up your machines eighty times instead of once."

"So we have to focus on eliminating set-up time" I suggested. "The time spend handling 400 finished armoires has been a hidden cost so far. We are going to find out whether building a daily or weekly batch will be more cost efficient than building and storing the entire build quantity."

As it turned out we determined that sawing and machining a weekly batch (20 sets at a time) made sense, while assembling and painting a daily batch (5 sets at a time) was the best solution.

We had just finished helping them set-up an entirely new small lot size manufacturing process when word arrived that a category 4 or 5 hurricane Katrina was bearing down on the gulf coast. They suggested that it was time for me to leave for safety sake (I agreed wholeheartedly).

I have often wondered about the person who drove me to the airport. After I turned in my rental car, I caught a ride to the airport in the rental car shuttle bus. I was the only one on board. Making small talk with the driver, I asked her if she was going to be leaving New Orleans to avoid the Hurricane. She laughingly replied "No, they always warn about another hurricane coming, but the storms never seem to hit us here. I've lived here all my life and they just get everyone all worked up over nothing." I hope she is OK.

The company I worked with was completely destroyed. I remember watching the news after the hurricane. Video being shot from helicopters showed the area along interstate Highway-10, right where the company was located. I am almost positive I saw the remains of their building and the mobile home that served as our kaizen war room. I am also sure that I saw armoires floating in the sea of rancid floodwater.

Illustration 17.1 Katrina Damage   Source: Google Images

Not your typical happy ending.

I felt for all the people affected with such devastation. These were hard working people, struggling as it was, only to be hit with an unfathomable natural disaster.

I was also convinced that I would never see payment for all the hard work I had done. I had hotel and airfare and rental car fees tied up in this project and had not yet invoiced them. I couldn't find it in my heart to send them a bill. It seemed like rubbing salt in the wound. But my financial advisor suggested that even if they could not pay, I had to submit an invoice for tax purposes, writing off the debt if unable to collect.

I finally wrote a letter explaining how I was discounting the invoice in light of the disaster they were facing. I let them know how badly I felt about having to invoice them at all, and that I would understand their not being able to submit payment.

A few weeks later I got an email from the owner of the company. His email was copied to his customers, vendors and employees as well as members of local and state and federal Government officials.

He had opened up his large estate to dozens of his employees. They had moved what equipment and materials they could salvage into a barn on his ranch, pitched a tent city on his acreage for employees and their families. His family was providing food, clean clothes, and bathing facilities for everyone while his team got back to the business of being in business (on a much smaller scale of course). This was not just a weekend camp out, this went on for months.

Disaster relief programs helped them get going again by providing low interest loans and grants.

He also mentioned in the email that he was trying to find ways to make good on debts incurred prior to the hurricane.

I wrote a newsletter to my 2,500 subscribers asking everyone to keep them in their prayers and relating the story of how large hearted this business man had been in reaching out to those in his company and community. He could have easily just run back to the relative safety of his estate and waited to collect the insurance money. Instead, he and his family extended themselves in a way many people might not.

I think that he is one of the greatest examples of self sacrifice I have ever seen.

Time went on, and I began projects with other clients and unless there was a news update about the disaster, I pretty much forgot about that little company in New Orleans.

Then six months later, a check arrived in the mail. The company had received insurance payment for their losses; amounting to enough for them to pay my fees.

Unbelievably; again this person went against the nature of most people to do the right thing.

This experience totally restored my faith in human kind. Whenever I hear news that makes me question my fellowman's right heartedness, I often replay this story in my mind. It reinforces for me that there are still trustworthy, empathetic, just and loving people in the world. I hope that I can demonstrate those same kinds of principles in my life.

Chapter Eighteen

A motorcycle in Japan

In an earlier story I made mention of the trip I made to Japan along with two other people from my company and our company president.

I am, and always have been an early morning person; it's probably why I've written six books. It's the only quiet thing I can do at 3:00 AM without waking up the family.

During my trip to Japan I also rose early. And I would find myself walking the streets of Japan before dawn seeking the nectar of the elusive coffee bean.

Not speaking Japanese was an enormous liability in this quest. At the time they did not have 7-11's or Circle K mini markets on every street corner like we do here in the US.

What they do have; and it took me a while to find this out, is; vending machines. The Japanese have found a way to meet the late night or early morning shopping needs of millions of people by installing vending machines on nearly every street corner. In fact, there are an estimated one million vending machines in Japan. These vending machines hold everything from cameras to writing pens, fresh fruit, and low and behold *coffee!*

Once I understood the Japanese symbol for coffee, I found that I could get chilled, heated, black, sweetened or any other variation of coffee in little V-8 sized cans. Life was good!

But coffee is not the reason for my story; I just thought I had better explain why I was walking the streets of Japan at 5:00 in the morning.

One morning, early in my visit, and before I had discovered the coffee vending system, I was walking along and came across a motorcycle sitting on the sidewalk. It was about the time that motorcycle designs were really changing. The upswept and gleaming chrome exhaust wrapped around curvaceous formed plastic, the stylish forks and handlebars were a far cry from the utilitarian design of the old Honda 350's that I had grown up with. This new bike definitely caught my attention as it sat there leaning back on it's' kick-stand.

Illustration 18.1 Motorcycle   Source: Google Images

As my eyes scanned the sleek frame, my head snapped back as I noticed that the key was in the ignition. I looked around thinking "Someone should tell a policeman about this!" But then I didn't speak Japanese, so what could I do? I shrugged my shoulders and continued my search for a hot cup of coffee.

A couple of blocks later I noticed a car parked alongside the curb. The windows were all rolled down; and while the steering wheel was on the other side, I couldn't help but notice the keys were dangling from the ignition.

"What is wrong with these people," I thought?

Later that morning I approached our tour guide and described to her what I had seen. She said "You must understand something about our culture. If we were to steal something from our neighbor, it would bring dishonor to our family for 400 years into the past and for 400 years into the future."

The emotional connection that these people have to community, parents, grandparents, children and grandchildren is something that we would do well to study.

I came to realize that this culture was one powerful reason why kaizen works so well in their country. They have been successful at implementing continuous improvement because people at every level of the organization want to provide a safe, secure, satisfying working environment not only for themselves, but for their children; and for their children's children. In the United States our managers (and workers) are trained to think *short term*. We tend to focus on the monthly P&L statement, thinking about the end of the week; the end of the month; the end of the quarter; the end of the fiscal year. Our competition is thinking about the end of this decade or the end of this century.

When you know this about our competition it makes you wonder if we will *ever* be able to achieve the same level of transformation; certainly not; unless we begin to retrain ourselves, our kids and our workforce to be long term thinkers.

Actual Cell Production	Blue Cell		
Revenue-Sales	$ 49,475.00		
Materials	$ 2,721.13	5.5%	
Subcontract	$ -	0.0%	
COG Override %	$ -	0.0%	
Value-Added Sales (VAS)	$ 46,753.88	100%	
Cell Daily Capacity Hours	48		
Cell Capacity Hours	1032	100%	
Production Hours	719	69.7%	
Produced Revenue	Monthly		Annually
Revenue	$ 49,475.00	15.2%	$ 593,700.00
Value-Added (VAS)	$ 46,753.88	18.5%	$ 561,046.50
ROA	$ 17,520.57	2.8%	$ 210,246.80
Profitability	$ 17,520.57	37.5%	$ 210,246.80
Actual Consumption	Monthly		Annually
Labor Factor	$ 15,321.76	18.2%	$ 183,861.12
MRF	$ 5,352.39	9.9%	$ 64,228.73
O&A	$ 6,761.43	9.9%	$ 81,137.21
Equip Factor	$ 1,000.00	1.3%	$ 12,000.00
PP Tax	$ 797.72	1.0%	$ 9,572.64
Total	$ 29,233.31	62.5%	$ 350,799.70
P&L			
VS Value-Added Sales	$ 46,753.88	100.0%	
VS Conversion Cost	$ 22,471.87	48.1%	
VS Gross Margin	$ 24,282.00	51.9%	
VS O&A Cost	$ 6,761.43	14.5%	
VS Profit	$ 17,520.57	37.5%	

Figure 18.1 Example P & L Statement

We tend to want instant gratification, and are often *unwilling* to spend the time and resources to invest in a long term vision with the objective of a positive *long term* outcome.

135

I did not get the impression that the Japanese people I met did this out of a sense of selfishness. By talking to the people right on the shop floor (through our translator) I came to appreciate that they came to work every day with the goal of making things better; not because they were going to get a $50 bonus or a bigger profit sharing check; but out of respect for the people who went before them (parents and grand-parents), and the people who will come after them.

They seemed very selfless and concerned that their great-great grand-child would have a job if they wanted one (and what made it even more amazing, was that in most cases, the child was not even born yet).

I think the rest of us can learn a lot from this approach.

Chapter Nineteen

The Roadmap

In the past decade we have seen Toyota, Volkswagon, and others catch-up and in some cases overtake the *Big Three* US automakers in worldwide sales, while at the same time we watched GM, Ford and Chrysler announce combined layoffs of 100,000's of workers.

My impression is that at trade shows and seminars I do not spend as much time as I used to trying to convince company leaders that they must initiate a change to the lean approach. Most managers recognize the need to adopt world class manufacturing principles.

The challenge has been to educate smaller "Make-to-Order" companies that there is an adaptable methodology used at OEM (original equipment manufacturers) like Toyota. These days I spend my time educating teams that there is a hybrid, yet tried and true, repeatable and sustainable roadmap to guide them during the transformation period.

My objective is to share insights about the proven path and the potential roadblocks that I've seen in the 150 or so companies that I've worked with. Companies do not have to "break a trail" any longer. The path to success is well known and documented.

The greatest risk that I see is that companies take a "Shot-gun" approach to their transformation.

A number of factors contribute to companies who struggle:

- Lack of direction or reliable roadmap

- Lack of education or concern by key players

- "Force fitting" the Toyota model; failure to consider the unique challenges of a high mix environment.

- Failure to ensure organizational Buy-in

As the graphic (roadmap) illustrates, there is a time tested route to World Class Performance. There are also many distractions, and detours along the way. These diversions can impede progress.

The most successful companies have learned (many times through the experience of others) to identify pitfalls and avoid roadblocks along the Lean journey.

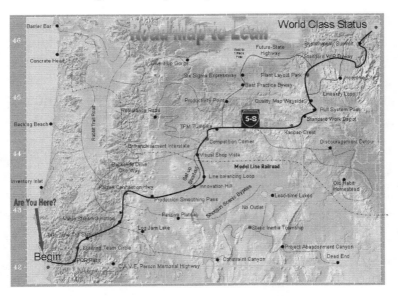

Illustration 19.1 Lean Roadmap   Source Lean Enterprise Training

138

Key steps in transforming a company to the Lean approach.

- Establish a steering team

- Conduct strategic planning session

- Train steering team in the disciplines of Lean (lean 101)

- Perform PQR (product-quantity-routing) analysis

- Identify value streams

- Select a value stream to use as a *model line*

- Select a kaizen team

- Train kaizen team in the disciplines of Lean (lean 101)

- Calculate model line takt time (hybrid takt time for job shops)

- Value stream map the model line

- Develop current state map

- Brainstorm alternatives to the current state

- Balance the line

- Assign standard work

- Establish standard WIP (inventory levels)

- Test the system (virtual cell) - document results

- Perform Set-up reduction events as required

- Apply 5-S (sort, straighten, shine, standardize, sustain)

- Apply TPM (total productive maintenance) techniques

- Establish visual signals

- Reduce paperwork

- Develop block layout

- Develop detailed layout

- Execute move

- Select next value stream and repeat

Chapter Twenty

Panic is the Mother of Invention

Working for a client in Alberta Canada about ten years ago we struggled to utilize the traditional value stream mapping process. I was at the desperate point of either developing a hybrid value stream mapping system or giving them their money back. Obviously I didn't want to give them back their money, so driven by a state of panic, I developed a completely new process for mapping high-mix, low volume manufacturing environments. Since that day I have tried exceptionally hard to break it, testing it by applying it within every imaginable type of business (including service organizations).

Our new value stream mapping system recognizes the fact that not all products have the same operator cycle time, machine cycle time, set-up time or yield. At Toyota, all cars get a windshield, a set of four tires, and seats. This is not always the case in job shops. Frequently there are products that do not use all processes. So the flow, takt time and pull systems must be set-up differently than in a pure assembly system.

To establish flow within job shops we have to try to *line balance* work content that varies significantly from part to part. *One piece flow* is the ideal, but not always realistic in a pure make-to-order environment.

Determining the "weighted average" Operator Cycle Time, as well as the weighted average Machine Cycle Time and Set-up

Time is a critical and often overlooked step in the traditional value stream mapping process.

For example, if a process like machining is used for four different product types; each requiring a slightly different process time, then it is not simply the average of all the times.

You must understand how the sales percentage of each can impacts the accuracy of true labor content. The goal must be to find an accurate weighted average "unit of work".

Let's say that hundreds of SKU's (part numbers) can be distilled down into four distinct part categories (A-B-C-D).

Example:

Product A = 50% of the sales volume. Product A requires 120 seconds to machine.

Product B = 20% of the sales volume. Product B requires 150 seconds to machine.

Product C = 5% of the sales volume. Product C requires 240 seconds to machine.

Product D = 25% of the sales volume. Product D requires 300 seconds to machine

In this case, the weighted average operator cycle time for a "unit of work" is 177 seconds. If you simply calculated the average of 120, 150, 240, 300, the result would be around 202 seconds. So you would end up with too many parts in WIP on average, you would assign too many people to the job, and possibly install too many machines as well. The same process is used to determine the MCT and Set-up times.

By appropriately balancing the line according to the weighted average Takt time, and Operator Cycle times you are better able to keep the flow, even in "make-to-order" shops.

Machining	Sales Percentage	Time Per unit	Weighted Average
OCT Type A	50.00%	120	
OCT Type B	20.00%	150	177
OCT Type C	5.00%	240	
OCT Type D	25.00%	300	
MCT Type A			
MCT Type B			
MCT Type C			0
MCT Type D			
Set-up type A			
Set-up type B			
Set-up type C			0
Set-up type D			

Figure 20.1   Example of value stream map process observation worksheet

It would be unrealistic to think that any program will work 100% of the time. We acknowledge that Pareto was correct in stating there is an 80-20% rule in almost every activity. We will still be better off if our system is designed to run perfectly 80% of the time, recognizing that 20% of the time it might not.

It's better to get the benefits 80% of the time. The unacceptable alternative is to run with no improvement 100% of the time. It is encouraging to see so many companies setting their sights high; moving their teams toward world class performance. There is obviously much work still to be done. We can learn much from each other. Best kept secrets could be our downfall. We need to help each other along this path. The journey is not always easy or intuitive, but with the right guidance and direction we can see our economy grow and thrive rather than shrink and waste away.

Chapter Twenty One

The Older I Got, the Smarter my Dad Got

Mark Twain said: "When I was a boy of fourteen, my father was so ignorant I could hardly stand to have the old man around. But when I got to be twenty-one, I was astonished at how much he had learned in seven years." In this the writer is able to distill something that we all experience in life. The passing of time makes us acutely aware of those in our lives, who in hindsight seem to have possessed wisdom far beyond our own.

Let's take a note from history.

Dr. W. Edwards Deming was a voice of wisdom and reason during the reformative years that followed World War II.

Like Mark Twain came to realize; we can see in hindsight that as time goes by, the truthfulness of Dr. Deming's words have become even more obvious.

He was; for lack of a kinder term "run out of town" by the US automakers as he warned of the exact result we see today. Dr. Deming subsequently found hearing ears in Japan. He was instrumental in the turnaround not only of Toyota, and Honda, but of Japan itself. He remains the only non Japanese person to be honored by receiving the "Second Order Medal of the Sacred Treasure" a presentation made by the Emperor of Japan himself. Dr. Deming has long since passed, but he leaves behind disciples, and I am proud to identify myself as such.

For the past twenty years I have tried my best to carry on Dr. Deming's message, sharing in his attempt to warn companies about an impending manufacturing and financial implosion; one that we are now all too familiar with.

Imagine that you are watching a stalled car stuck on a set of train tracks as a fully loaded freight train bears down on it at full speed. You would try everything in your power to try to get the train to stop. Dr. Deming was screaming at the top of his lungs at the train (American Business Leaders) who seemed happily ignorant of the fact that they were heading for unavoidable disaster. The truth is; it was not unavoidable if only they were willing and able to change direction. But because of inertia, fast moving trains cannot change direction quickly. Because of organizational inertia, businesses in motion (using old business models) tend to stay in motion (using old methodologies).

Illustration 21.1 Dr. Deming   Source: deming.org

For those who paid attention to Dr. Deming, they could see the economic catastrophe coming. For the past twenty five years his disciples were screaming at the top of their lungs; but very few business leaders wanted to hear it. Then we were forced to watch the economic collision unfold before us like a horrific and slow motion train wreck.

I am not alone in experiencing the frustration of trying to sound the alarm while greedy stock market players, short sighted CEO's, CFO's and a good many other management types have ignored Dr. Deming, choosing instead to focus on short term earnings. They have been myopic in their quest for *quarterly bonuses* and other forms of personal gain, all while driving their own companies into the ditch and into possible extinction. All the while expecting the very workers whose livelihoods they put at risk, and shareholders they fleece to feel sorry for them; bail them out and pay them a bonus to boot.

There are many of us (including my competitors) who have for years been preaching at the tops of our lungs.

Dr. Deming had to deal with this same frustration for decades before his passing. His disciples have inherited his mission and his frustration. But just because he was frustrated, he did not stop trying to remedy the problems of his day. And neither can we.

A doctor cannot give up on a seriously ill patient just because a patient may earlier have ignored advice against abusing drugs, cigarettes and alcohol. The doctor has an obligation to salvage the patient's quality of life. He must continue to help turn around a bad situation if possible. Dr. Deming's disciples have a similar obligation. I hope that I have taken my obligation seriously.

Recently I have watched other Lean Manufacturing disciples walk away from the operating theater. This economy has forced many of my consulting brethren (my competitors) in this battle into more traditional manufacturing roles or into early retirement. Did they give up? Did their patients give up? Should I give up?

I have had to intellectually wrestle with myself about where my obligation begins and ends. I have authored five other books on the subject of manufacturing, lean, six sigma and continuous improvement. I have trained tens of thousands. Can I consider my work complete?

Illustration 21.2   Lean Manufacturing and Six Sigma for the Small Shop

I have watched the number of people attending tradeshow seminars and workshops dwindle. Attendee rosters seem to mirror and react to the cyclical nature of the stock market.

Have we trained them all? I don't think so. Are there more patients out there who want help? I have to hope and believe so. Dr. Deming didn't stop, and I can't either.

So I will continue to preach the message. And hope that my fellow trainers (competitors) will do the same. There are just too many people who need help. I hope that instead of reaching the point of giving into the frustration, we use this pivotal moment in time to regroup, rethink and restore the unique capabilities that we share. I hope that we can all take a larger lesson from Japan, not just that they adopted Lean Manufacturing, but that they pulled together to change their situation. We saw it again after the massive earthquake, tsunami and resulting human suffering this year (2011).

After World War II the Japanese people had every reason to feel like giving up. Their towns were in ruin, they were occupied by a foreign country, they had virtually no natural resources, they lacked any manufacturing capability and they had few markets for their products. It's easy to see how they might have just given up, forfeited their future to the hopelessness and helplessness that shrouded their situation at that moment in time.

But Dr. Deming helped them, and they refused to die on the symbolic operating table. They made the necessary behavioral changes; they worked together; they educated each other; and they shared *best practices* as they were discovered. They coached and trained the next generation. They challenged everything that they had ever done; they found improvements, and then challenged themselves to find yet a better way the very next day.

Since beginning my consulting career I have worked with over 150 companies. We can conservatively measure the combined savings in the hundreds of millions of dollars. I don't think it would be presumptuous to state that these companies are stronger; they are not just surviving, but are thriving because of the work that I have done. I guess that's why I have to keep doing it. I am motivated by the positive example of others.

I feel like the old country doctor who just can't stop doing what he's doing, because eventually he knows that he might save a life.

Actual lives may not be at stake here, but livelihoods are. We have an obligation to each other to do the very best we can. I have an obligation to share with as many business minded individuals as will listen; lessons learned, case studies and best practices from the nearly five hundred kaizen and continuous improvement projects that I've conducted since beginning my career. And you have the same obligation.

If you are a consultant keep working hard for your patients (clients).

If you are a manager, get a check up (lean assessment).

If you are on the finance team, learn about Lean Accounting.

If you are an in-house lean coordinator, continue your education.

If you are a front line leader or manager, demand that your company provide your teams with education in the disciplines of Lean Thinking.

Chapter Twenty Two

Machines do not a World Class Company Make

President George W. Bush paid Oregon a visit in February of 2002. He came here because even prior to the economic meltdown, Oregon was 48th out of 50 states; we had some of the highest unemployment and slowest economic growth in the nation.

He spoke at length about the sagging Northwest economy; using Oregon as a poster child, as if to say; "This is what a State looks like when it is stuck in a depressed economic condition."

His answer?

Offer companies tax incentives to buy new equipment.

This proposal later became law. Has it helped?

I am not *throwing rocks* at the President, or his idea, and this is not a political statement. The law helped some firms who needed financial incentives to upgrade their equipment.

However, after spending time in nearly every state, visiting hundreds of companies, I believe that the answer is not in more equipment or new mechanical technologies. The answer instead lies in changed behaviors.

The reason customers look elsewhere is that they find suppliers who behave more competitively and offer greater value and quicker response times.

This is not a chicken-and-the-egg kind of problem. If we want customers to seek our services and products, we must first demonstrate an ability to satisfy their desire for value, quality, and availability.

Getting new equipment is very sexy, but it won't gain you sustainable business unless your company uses it to behave as a world-class organization; capitalizing on the talent of your people and the capacity and capability of your buildings and supply chain. In short, increased sales do not necessarily follow the purchase of more or new equipment.

So what is the answer?

In nearly every workshop I teach, we perform a short exercise to help the audience define the term "world class". We want to be able to distinguish the characteristics that sets *good* apart from *great*.

We start by generating a list of athletes who set themselves apart as world class examples in their chosen sport. The list almost always includes names like; Mohammed Ali, Michael Jordan and Wayne Gretsky.

After developing a list of 10-15 names, we return to each name and add a word adjective (description) that in the minds of the audience sums up and captures the essence of what made that person a world class performer.

Words like; drive, dedication, charisma, talent, coaching, desire usually make the list.

Then we have the team develop a list of companies that they consider world class. Microsoft, Harley Davidson, Honda and others are typically offered as examples.

We then ask the group to identify the one word descriptors that capture the essence of why these companies are considered world class. Without fail; after a few moments of silence the group always looks around the room at each other simultaneously arriving at the same conclusion; the list is really the same one developed earlier, when describing world class athlete characteristics: talent, coaching, drive, consistency…

Never, in the four hundred times I've done that exercise (not even when we did it at NIKE) has anyone ever said that the reason Michael Jordan was world class depended on the shoes he wore, or the brand of basketball he played with, or the arena he played in. Jordan could have played barefoot, with a soccer ball, on a dirt covered playground and his performance against similarly outfitted competitors would likely have still been viewed as world class.

It has less to do with the machines we have, and *more* to do with the behaviors of the teams we lead; and how our teams use the equipment we have (new or old).

Chapter Twenty Three

Poka-Yoke; The end of Quality Control?

I make mistakes.

I am not an idiot.

At least I have friends who tell me that I am not.

Yet I make mistakes from time to time.

Regardless; after discovering that I have made a mistake, I still feel like an idiot.

I'm not the only one. It seems like I am surrounded by mistake prone people at times. Recently my rental car agency forgot to reserve a car for me, and I had to pay $125 for a forty mile cab ride. I am *sure* that the rental car agency employees are not idiots, although in the heat of the moment I quite likely would have sworn to that fact.

So, idiot proofing a process would not stop good people from making mistakes. It would only stop idiots from making mistakes. Since most of the mistake prone people I know are not idiots, we need a better way to mistake proof processes and a better name for the process of mistake proofing.

Murphy 's Law states: "If something can go wrong it will."

Does that mean that efforts to mistake proof processes are simply exercises in futility? Are we only delaying the inevitable? Will the mistake happen whether preventative measures are in place or not? Is there in actuality nothing we can do to guarantee that mistakes are avoided? These are just a couple of the questions we hope to answer. The answer needs to be a definitive "no".

In our workshops we have participants view a sixty second video. They are given the simple assignment of counting the number of times two soccer balls are passed between two groups of people. At the end of the exercise, there is usually a wide variety of opinion about the number of times the ball was passed. We also ask if anyone saw anything unusual in the video. About twenty percent of the people will admit to having seen a gorilla. Everyone else snickers and wags their head in disbelief that their fellow participants could be so mistaken. As we watch the video a second time, everyone sees a person dressed in a gorilla costume slowly walk into the scene, stop, face the camera, beat his chest and then calmly walk out of the scene. The group that did not see the gorilla during the first viewing sits gap-jawed at the realization that they missed it entirely. The purpose of the exercise is then explained. Humans are really not very good at multi-tasking. We can easily be fooled, our eyes deceive us. That's why optical illusions work. Humans are not good at inspection. We often miss large things (like a gorilla) when we are focused on other things.

In fact here is an exercise that you can try for yourself. I am going to give you an assignment to inspect for a defect. Go back to the previous paragraph (the entire paragraph is in italics) and look for a defect. Take no more than one minute to count the defects. The defect you are looking for is represented by the

155

letter "F". Count the number of times that the letter "F" appears in the paragraph (count both lower case and capital letters).

How many did you count? Most people will miss about half of the "F's". Why? Because our brains trick us.

We see the "F's" that sound like an "F".

But when the "F" follows an "O" (as in the word "of"), then the "F" sounds more like a "V".

If we do not hear an "F", we are less likely to count the "F".

There are actually eighteen "F's" in the paragraph. So what does all this prove?

You could have one hundred inspectors inspecting one hundred percent of your product, and you could still not guarantee one hundred percent accuracy.

No amount of inspection will eliminate defects. Humans are poor inspectors. Therefore, we must eliminate the potential for defects rather than trying to find defects.

Even if we reduce the probability of defects to one in a thousand, we are accepting the fact that at some point a defect will be produced, in effect saying "After all we are only human". We must therefore "human proof" the process.

Reducing defects to one out of a thousand, would result in a 99.9% accuracy rate; still unacceptable. For example; if airlines accepted a 99.9% rate as their quality target for accident free travel, there would be 240 air traffic accidents everyday.

Hospital nurseries satisfied with a 99.9% quality rating would hand over 12 babies to the wrong parents everyday.

In order to eliminate airline accidents and medical mistakes, these industries have had to incorporate mistake proofing techniques. Poka-yoke (pronounced: Poh-kah yoh-kay) is a Japanese term referring to "human induced" mistake proofing.

In addition to Poka-Yoke, another Japanese term "Jidoka" refers to elimination of "machine induced" defects.

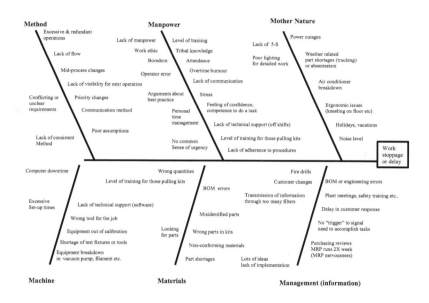

Illustration 23.1   Ishikawa Diagram example

Looking at an Ishikawa Diagram (also known as the cause and effect diagram) you will notice that there are six primary potential causes for any effect. Each of these inputs begins with the letter "M" as a memory aid. Manpower, Method, Materials,

157

Mother-Nature (the environment), Management (information) and Machines. Jidoka deals primarily with "machine induced" defects. Poka-Yoke addresses the other five inputs to the process.

As long as we have variables in a process we will have defects. I used to run a laser cutting machine. It still fascinates me that we could cut a ¼" inch thick sheet of stainless steel with a beam of light focused to about the diameter of a human hair. But when laser cutting technology was in its infancy the process was fraught with variability. This variability led to enormous defect potential, huge waste rates, and unacceptable rework costs. We identified seventeen variables including; material type, material condition, material thickness, focal length, feed rate, humidity and on, and on. It was like trying to juggle seventeen balls at once. There was little chance of a human successfully managing all the things that could go wrong. Until we were able to eliminate the variables, we were going to have defects.

Through the use of Poka-Yoke we were able to minimize or eliminate the effect of one variable after another, until the process was no longer prone to generate mistakes.

Shigeo Shingo, one of the key architects of the Toyota (and in a larger sense the Japanese) turnaround in quality and productivity wrote about the discovery and development of mistake proofing in his book: "Zero Quality Control, Source Inspection and the Poka-yoke system." (Productivity Press) In his book, Mr. Shingo details seven stages, seven levels of understanding, seven principles based on evidence that led him to the belief that traditional quality control techniques (including statistical process control) can only detect a defect after it is generated. Of course it can also statistically predict with varying degrees of certainty the number of future defects that will be produced.

Mr. Shingo was seeking a method of preventing any defect from being produced in the first place. In his mind, to use a control chart to discover or predict defects was unacceptable.

The seven stages of understanding that Mr. Shingo wrote about are as follows:

Stage 1: SQC (traditional statistical tools used to detect process variation and defects).

Stage 2: Encounter with Poka-yoke method (initial experiments with mistake proofing).

Stage 3: Encounter with successive- (or self-) check; what we now refer to as NOV (next operator verification, or the buddy check system); having the next operator perform a visual or functional test as a part of his standard work.

Stage 4: Realization that sampling inspections only rationalize inspection procedures. (This is counter-intuitive; Mr. Shingo came to realize that as long as there was the potential for defects, there needed to be 100% inspection rather than a sampling plan for inspection.) The key is that the method of inspection should be automatic if possible, requiring no human intervention.

Stage 5: Encounter with source inspection (inspection needs to be built into the process rather than "added on" as a function designed to detect a defect(s) only after one or more have been produced.) This may even require the machine "set-up" to be inspected prior to running a first piece.

Stage 6: Realization that "Zero Defects" are possible. Through personal experience, working with numerous teams, Mr. Shingo saw evidence that Poka-yoke techniques implemented in manufacturing process previously fraught with variability and defects were able to run month after month without generating defects. At this stage, control charts become not only non-value added activities, but nearly worthless information.

Stage 7: Establishment of Zero Quality Control. Acknowledging that humans are not infallible. Using automated source inspection for 100 percent of the production. Minimizing the time required to discover and remedy abnormalities.

So what are some of the techniques in the Poka-yoke tool box?

	Saw	Press Brake	Frame weldment	Mid Assy
Specification	Part print	Flat Pattern	Assy (Weld) Print	Spec sheet (options)
Current estimate of rework	5%	1%	4%	0%
Inspection method	Tape	Calipers, protractor	Tape, pin gauge	Tape, Visual, jigs
Inspection Frequency	They measure the set-up not the part	Sampling plan	100%	100%
Defect potential	1. Wrong length 2. Wrong detail 3. Wrong material 4. Wrong part count	1.Wrong location 2.Wrong orientation 3.Wrong hole size 4.Insufficient weld 5.Missed welds	1.Wrong part location 2.Wrong orientation 3.Wrong hole size 4.Insufficient weld 5.Missed welds 6. Wrong weld location	1. Wrong location 2. Wrong orientation 3. Wrong hole size 4. Insufficient weld 5. Missed welds 6. Loose bolts,fittings
Potential Cause	1a. Operator error 1b. print error 1c. BOM error	1a. Operator error 1b. print unclear 2a. locating part on wrong side of line. 3a. 3b. 3c.	1a. Operator error 1b. Print unclear 1c. Locating part on wrong side of line.	
Ideas for improvement		1a1. Training 1a2. Standardized prints 1b1. B size prints 2a1. Parts presentation	1a1. Training 1a2. Poka-Yoke 1b1. Training 1b2. Color code 1b3. Overlay template	

Figure 23.1 Example Quality Map

The first rule of 'kaizen' (continuous improvement) is that you must understand the process. The first step in Poka-yoke is to conduct a quality mapping event. Quality mapping is similar to value stream mapping, which documents the current state of information and material flow through each administrative or manufacturing processes.

Quality mapping differs from value stream mapping in that rather than focusing on operator cycle times or set-up times; you are identifying and documenting the variables in each process. In other words; what are the potential defects at each step of the process. Not what you could find; because you can find a problem anywhere, but rather, what defect could you *induce* at each step.

Figure 23.1 shows a simplified example of a quality map. Notice that the same six questions are asked at each stage of the process.

- What is the specification (how do you know that you are making it correctly?)

- What is the inspection method (visual, dimensional, attribute, etc..?)

- What is the inspection frequency (sampling plan, first and last, first article…?)

- What are the defect potentials (what defects could be induced at this step?)

- What are the potential causes of each of these defect types?

161

- What ideas are there for elimination of the defect potentials?

As the team collects this data they may determine the most likely candidates for further observation, they may also begin brainstorming ideas for possible poka-yoke devices or defect prevention techniques.

In one Poka-Yoke project, the team identified a common defect related to the installation of circuit board *stand-offs* (a stand-off is a double ended piece of hardware which allows a circuit board to be installed at an engineered distance from the computer chassis; allowing airflow between to two circuit boards or providing clearance from a mounting surface.

Illustration 23.2   Standoff hardware

One operator was responsible for installing a number of such hardware pieces. These stand-offs were usually installed as a set of four. One such set of stand-offs were 1.032 inches in length. Another set used elsewhere in the cabinet was 1.063 inches in length. Left to his or her own devices, eventually, an operator was sure to mix the hardware or install it in the wrong place.

The team examined the process and determined that this variable was extremely likely to create the need for rework. So they separated one of the sets of stand-offs, reassigning this portion of *standard work* to a different assembly operator. This eliminated one variable in the process.

Although this supplier was not in charge of design, the best solution would have been to standardize the components to be identical; then it wouldn't matter where any piece of hardware was placed. Their solution to separate the hardware installation between two operators was the best they could do.

Before they made the switch, they had explored other alternatives including color coding the stand-offs. For example purchasing standoffs having different colored plating (bright zinc as opposed to yellow zinc plating) to minimize the chance of an error. But color coding still allowed the opportunity for a mistake. Since some employees might be color blind, they determined reassigning the work was a better solution.

By implementing this and other simple changes, the group lowered their DPMO (defects per million opportunities) from 24,000 to 2,400 saving an estimated $400,000 per year in service and reclaim costs.

One of our investment casting clients had been dealing with a 6% waste rate. This client made lots of different kinds of products for the medical industry, including artificial knees, hips and other such products.

Investment casting requires that an exact copy (mold) of a part first be made out of wax, assembled onto a larger mold with up to 20 similar wax castings. The mold is then coated numerous times with a ceramic material, dried and then "de-waxed" by melting the wax out of the mold in a 1,200 degree pre-heat chamber.

This leaves behind an empty shell that will be filled with molten metal. Once cooled, the ceramic casing is then cleaned off the casting.

This company had a process that generated six defects out of each hundred molds. The molds would develop cracks which would then fail while having the molten metal poured into them.

Illustration 23.3 Artificial Knee (raw casting)

As you can imagine, having 2,700 degree molten metal running out of a cracked mold and onto the floor (actually into a sand pit) was a substantial safety hazard, as well as a multi-million dollar waste problem.

The team found through an examination of the quality map that one of the 150 variables in their process was related to two different types of wax being used to create a mold.

Reclaimed (previously melted) wax was used for the "gating" or for the non consumable portion of the mold. While new or "virgin" wax was used for the actual component (knee or hip).

Reclaimed wax was used to provide pathways for the molten metal to move through the mold and enter the component cavity.

By conducting a relatively simple test, they found that the virgin wax melted at a lower temperature than reclaimed wax. Due to the required positioning of the mold in the wax evacuation furnace (autoclave), the difference in melting temperature allowed the virgin wax to melt, expand and potentially crack the mold long before the reclaimed wax began to melt.

Instead of trying to develop a method of detecting cracks (defects), they designed a process to eliminate cracks. At the same time, they did not want to bear to cost of using virgin wax for the entire mold, so they tested and proved that engineering a *vent* into each mold allowed for expansion of the virgin wax while allowing sufficient time to melt the reclaimed wax.

Problem solved. No further inspection required. This resulted in a three million dollar per year savings; and they got a significant safety improvement to boot.

I am sure that we have all heard the horror stories of surgeons removing the wrong kidney, or operating on the wrong leg when someone is undergoing knee replacement surgery.

Possible mistakes are being minimized by hospital staff by having knee replacement patients (prior to being anesthetized) write "NO!", or some other impossible to misinterpret signal in big, bold, permanent marker ink on the knee not requiring attention.

Now when the patient is sedated, his or her message is still visible and avoids the chance of a mistake.

When automobile manufacturers began designing cars to burn unleaded fuel, they implemented a poka-yoke device into each new car. In an effort to eliminate the chance of someone pumping leaded gas into a car meant to burn unleaded gasoline, they changed the orifice size. Fuel companies adapted the size of the nozzle as well.

Memory stick (jump-drives), USB cables, DVD's and computer disks have a built in Poka-yoke device. If you attempt to insert a disc backward or upside down, it will either not fit, or the machine will kick it out. These are examples of poka-yoke devices.

Illustration 23.4 Machined parts

Due to the "soft tool" nature of today's modern *small lot size* shops, there is much greater flexibility; but process control is more challenging than if everything were "hard tooled' as in the case of large quantity stamping. Machine shops often design locating pins or blocking devices into a die, or lockout mechanisms into tools, preventing operators from inserting parts upside down, backwards or in the wrong sequence. It may be more difficult to perfectly Poka-yoke soft tooling, but reduction of process variation is almost always possible if best practices are employed.

In an effort to minimize machine set-ups, an example of variation elimination was developed and implemented by one Press Brake (forming machine) kaizen team. For years each operator had maintained their own "little black book" within which each operator stored his or her own "secret" set-up techniques. The little black book was then squirreled away deep within their locked tool box. The team decided to standardize their set-ups. They selected the best method after inviting everyone's input. Then they developed standard practices for pre-setting the tooling. As expected, this improved set-up times, but it also eliminated *operator to operator* variation, an unexpected benefit was discovered when they realized that the number of adjustments and scrap rate had also been significantly reduced.

Rather than designing and constructing expensive and complicated (often called a *Rube Goldberg)* mechanisms in an attempt to ensure part quality, focus instead on reducing the variation instead.

Self-Operating Napkin

Illustration 23.5 Rube Goldburg cartoon   Source: Department of Agriculture

The most successful solutions are often the result of simple and low cost process modifications (suggested by operators) as opposed to complex and pricey engineered poka-yoke devices.

Where a device makes sense, mechanical and industrial engineers can certainly help, but *simple* is best. The tendency is to over-engineer a solution rather than capitalize on the intellectual capacity of the people actually performing the work.

Get the team involved. Have them examine the process and identify the areas of weakness. Have them ask themselves, "What could possibly go wrong?" And "Of all the things that could possibly go wrong which are the most likely to happen" And "How could we put measures in place that would make if very hard for someone to make a mistake?"

In the sport of boxing, the term "robust" means; 'not easily knocked off your feet.' When applied to manufacturing processes the term *robust* has the same connotation. The process is not easily knocked out of control or cannot easily produce a defect.

We have recently seen a transformation occurring in the Quality Assurance field. Directors of Quality are becoming less like "quality police", and more like "quality educators" helping teams learn to study the process and develop the *power of observation* muscle, helping them to recognize variation; coaching them to implement poka-yoke techniques to eliminate the variables one by one.

Being lean (being world class) is not just about making parts *fast*. It is about making *good parts fast*, and with the least amount of waste, including the elimination of non-value added activities related to rework, rejects and reclaim.

Poka-yoke is just one tool of many in the Lean Manufacturers tool kit. On its own it will not make you world class, but coupled with other fundamental tools such as set-up reduction, 5-S, Pull systems, the application of Takt time, balanced lines, standard work, standard WIP (inventory) and a facility layout that fosters flow, companies are beginning to recognize enormous benefits on the bottom line.

Chapter Twenty Four

Poker is a Zero Sum Game

I had just arrived home from a manufacturing conference in Nevada when a publisher, called me with the request to submit an article on how Lean Manufacturing can help companies forced to operate within a new (slower) economy.

Having just spent time in Vegas, I couldn't help thinking of how running business is a little like playing poker. Both endeavors take place within an environment that is influenced by a principle known in mathematics as the 'zero-sum' rule.

Illustration 24.1 Painting: Dogs Playing Poker   by Cassius Marcellus Coolidge

Allow me to explain. Poker is a zero sum game because if 5 people all bring $20 to the table, it is a $100 game. At the end of the game, there is still $100 on the table, although someone will probably take home more than they came with, and someone will thus go home with less.

If someone *wins* at poker, someone else *has to lose;* there is no other mathematic possibility or result. This in essence is the Zero Sum Principle.

Business is like the game of poker, because if one company wins a customer account, then the chances are very good that another supplier has lost the business; a proposal, or a customer account. Like the finite number of poker chips on the game table, there are only so many potential contracts out there.

Of course we always want to be on the right side of this equation. How can we make the decision to buy from us a *no-brainer* for the customer? How can we make the *Cost-Availability-Quality* buying decision drivers favor our organization to *such* a degree that the customer can't see a viable alternative to buying *our* product or service? And by the way; how do we provide that *buying* decision at a level of profitability for our company that enables and ensures growth, while remaining environmentally responsible?

One word: Lean.

From my first day working in the precision sheet metal industry, I was educated that bigger is better. The larger the batch size, the more economical and profitable the sales order. It was a shock when in the 1980's our customers began requesting weekly deliveries rather than monthly batches.

It wasn't long before we realized that profits were eroding with each reduced lot size. We searched for a tool (a tourniquet) to stop the bleeding, but it appeared to us that there was no such device.

What worked for larger companies didn't seem to work for us.

Finally we took part in a pilgrimage to Japan in hopes of finding how companies like Toyota had approached the many issues that we were now facing.

We spent twelve days, riding bullet trains the length and breadth of Japan; visiting twenty different companies.

We visited auto manufacturing plants as well as vending machine manufacturers, and companies of every size and description. Yet again, the solutions applied in the Japanese shops we visited fell short when we tried to apply them to our Job Shop.

No one seemed to have the *magic bullet;* a one-size-fits-all answer.

And yet, some of the consultants we talked to kept dogmatically insisting that if we did not adopt the Toyota Production System exactly as Toyota had, there was no hope for us, and we might as well go purchase a rope and a rafter, and hang ourselves.

Through trial and error, and after a few year of struggling, we finally had a breakthrough when we came to realize that there is no one-size-fits-all template that could be applied when dealing with a strictly 'make-to-order' business like ours. Was this reason enough to throw up our arms in defeat?

No! The path to *lean,* works for companies of all sizes; and regardless of customer order patterns.

We simply had to apply a hybrid approach when dealing with an order file that had limited predictability.

At the risk of oversimplification, the answer lies in the realization that *lean* is a whole host of tools that can be applied (and in some cases modified) within any business model.

The challenge is to select the correct tools to apply in your individual organizations or 'value streams'. I am not suggesting that the lean tools be viewed as a *buffet* from which we can select only the tools that make us feel good. Some tools are hard to implement, yet critical to the World Class transformation of a company.

The strength of job shops lay in their ability to react in a nimble nature with nearly infinite flexibility. The capability to turn on a dime when demand requires it is what endears Mom-and-Pop shops to customers. One Piece Flow, Takt-Time and Pull are fine in a pure assembly process, but in a *make to order* environment, a hybrid approach must often be employed to avoid the risk of losing flexibility.

By applying these fundamental tools well, you will position yourself to respond quicker to changing customer needs.

The *Zero Sum* principle is unforgiving.

Make sure that you come to the *table* ready and *able* to play. That requires training and practice.

Chapter Twenty Five

Bigger is not always better

A search of the internet will yield 1000's of websites dedicated to every imaginable improvement program developed by man. Business sections of book stores are full of *self help* text books. It's terrific that there is so much interest and encouragement to help companies achieve their world class vision. But there is only so much time in the day. How are we to know what approach to take?

Each consultant, website or book seems to figuratively wave a different flag (approach); as if it were the best (if not only) choice. Yet there are thousands of consultants, books and websites; each seeming to tout a slightly different approach.

Adding to the complexity is the fact that every couple of years a new approach is invented. Or someone modifies or blends together a number of approaches; creating yet another variation.

The resulting confusion has led to a kind of 'agnosticism'; a belief that if there were a clear answer, everybody would know it. This condition leads many to take a *wait and see* attitude as if the path should be immediately evident, with irrefutable evidence that *this way* is the *only way*.

In the confusion, confounded companies often do nothing.

The challenge for consultants as well as companies seeking to improve is to be able to distinguish between *tools* and *objectives*. Lean manufacturing, Just in Time, the Toyota Production System, Six Sigma, all these *tools* exist and can be used to help achieve the *objective* of being World Class, but the tools themselves are not the objective.

Being viewed by your customer (and your competitors) as the world class *standard* by which all other competitors are judged is the goal. Finding the right tools to get you there will vary with each company.

Exploring the vast number of tools available and applying the right one at the right time is the responsibility of the leaders in each organization. There is certainly no shortage of material written on the subject. In spite of this, or maybe *because* of this, there seems to be an overwhelming number of companies taking a "we'll see" attitude about the matter. Their thoughts may be that 'this too shall pass'.

Maybe they are waiting for the 'Lean' fad to pass, like the pet rock or hula-hoop. After all, management programs like this usually fade after time. Or maybe, in an effort to justify their own business services, consultants have created the illusion that the lean transformation process is more complicated than it really is. Companies may be waiting for the distillation (boiling down to a few key elements) or simplification of the Lean approach. Like; "We'll wait for the movie to come out."

Over the last three decades there have been additions, refinements, re-labeling and re-packaging of the techniques applied at Toyota, however, a few fundamental tools have been constant and are being applied alongside improvement techniques like Six Sigma and others.

Tools like set-up reduction, line balancing, pull systems, running a *paced* line (known as Takt Time) have shown remarkable results when applied within companies (including job shops) the world over to improve performance regardless of industry, company size, geographic location, or customer ordering patterns.

Value Stream Mapping is another fundamental tool. But here as well, there are differences in the way OEM's and Job Shops should approach the use of this tool.

You would never permit your family to begin a journey through hostile jungle with a tattered paper map, full of holes and erasures. There may have been changes in river flow patterns, village locations and new land features. For the safety of your family and yourself, you would do your best to prepare for the journey with the best equipment, perhaps including a GPS loaded with the latest topographical maps.

So, why do so many companies continue to use value stream mapping techniques from the past. The faithful old roll of butcher paper hanging in the kaizen war room may have worked perfectly at Toyota, but most job shops are finding it difficult and costly to maintain, hard to understand, too easily destroyed and often inaccurate due to process improvements. Or the frequency of changes in order files or patterns.

One of the fundamental tools in the lean manufacturing tool box has been value stream mapping. For the past few years the *Learning to See* methodology has been utilized with great success within companies the world over. Mike Rother, John Shook and their team deserve much praise for bringing this process to kaizen teams (myself included) in an easy to understand fashion.

New and improved value stream mapping methodologies, specifically developed for high mix, low volume environments can benefit your team's efforts.

Like anything else, a head start can be a nearly irreversible advantage. Many organizations have used value stream mapping and other tools in the Lean approach to gain a marketable advantage in performance, in the process pulling ahead of their competition in terms of market share gains, productivity and financial performance.

A 'Pure Toyota' approach works very well in assembly operations. It can be more challenging to apply within pure *make-to-order* or *engineer-to-order* manufacturing environments. These organizations need to retain their ability to respond quickly to the dynamics of their customers unique order patterns and often non-existent forecasting systems.

As customers become more and more demanding in regard to shorter lead times, smaller lot sizes, and reduced product life cycles, any 'job shop' could benefit by incorporating a few key techniques developed and perfected at Toyota.

Inventory reduction through the use of increased *Product Flow Velocity* can be recognized even in Mom-and-Pop shops. By taking time to learn and apply these tools, your organization can move to the next plateau (level of performance).

We must avoid being dogmatic in our approach. We cannot expect that the exact tools will work in every company. Sometimes the answer is not one-piece-flow. Sometimes it must be one-kit-flow, or one-pallet-flow, or one-truckload-flow. The idea is to make progress toward the "ideal" of one-piece flow.

Any improvement is worthwhile. My message would be "Don't wait for perfection. Get started!"

If you wait six months, you will be six months behind. If we are to survive as an economy, we must be able to compete with very nimble and capable companies (and countries) who have had years of experience in getting lean. To match their performance, we will have to have a very low *value added ratio*.

Value added ratio is the difference between value added and non-value-added activities in your processes.

For example, if it takes two minutes to perform a task, but the box of parts ahead of your process contains one hundred units, then there is two hundred minutes of work waiting for every minute of work performed. The value added activity is therefore 1% or a ratio of 1:100

The shorter the dwell time of products or services, the lower the value added ratio will be. World class companies are focusing their efforts on achieving a value added ratio of 1:10. For every minute of value added effort, no more than ten minutes of dwell time or delay will be permitted.

Not many companies have achieved this level. I would say that when I first visit companies who are just starting down the lean manufacturing path, their value added ratio is closer to 1:200.

So, bigger is *not* better. The *smaller* the value added ratio is; then the *higher* the percentage of value added is; from the customers perspective.

Chapter Twenty Six

Scraping the Barnacles

Illustration 26.1   Barnacles

What do barnacles and manufacturing waste have to do with each other? Let me explain.

The Acorn barnacle is a small crustacean, roughly the size of a quarter when full grown.   It attaches itself to a host (for example; a ship) for life. The adhesive properties in the cement excreted by this creature are amazing. The excreted compound can bond the barnacle to its host with 7,200 pounds per square inch holding force.   One barnacle could support the weight of a full sized pickup if you could figure out a way to connect it.

Living in Newport Oregon and having owned a fishing boat for seven years, I can personally attest to the tenacity of these little creatures. Every year, after fishing season I would have to prepare my boat for winter storage. This included scraping the hull free of thousands of barnacles.

While it was a good deal of work, it was really little more than a nuisance to me. To the shipping industry however, barnacles represent a huge financial liability.

Estimated costs associated with speed loss and increased fuel consumption resulting from these mollusks' growing on the hulls of ships is estimated to be $1.4 billion per year problem. Referred to as "Fouling," these barnacles contribute to increased fuel costs of up by 7 percent after only one month and 44 percent after six months.

The traditional remedy has included *dry docking* the ship, then scraping and sandblasting the barnacles off the hull. The cleaned surface is often covered with a coating of antifouling agent; chemically enhanced paint, to discourage the barnacles' return.

The challenge for shipping companies is that the barnacles are hidden below the water line. Out of sight; out of mind. The only indication that fouling has occurred is the vessel's reduced performance. Could our companies be fouled; slowed down or consuming resources unnecessarily; by barnacle-like behaviors? How can we "scrape the hulls" of our organization to ensure smooth, unrestricted, and cost-efficient advancement?

Barnacles can be likened to the non-value-added activities we perform every day. During a recent kaizen event at a client company in Nevada, the team performed a value-added observation. The initial observation showed that the operator was able to spend just over twenty (20) percent of his day in a value-adding mode. It wasn't that he wasn't working hard, he just had so many non-value added things to do that nearly eighty (80) percent of his time was deemed to be providing no value; from the customer perspective.

After the kaizen (a Japanese term meaning continuous improvement) event, the team had rearranged his work area, developed new work standard, and set his operation up to run at takt time (manufacturing rhythm based on available time divided by demand), this worker produced three times as many parts. He now spends well over sixty (60) percent of his time in value-added activities (still room for improvement).

Sequence	Activity	Clock	Labor	VA	NNVA	UNVA
1	Move parts from last job	0:00:25	0:00:50			x
2	Retrieve paperwork for next job	0:07:44	0:15:28		x	
3	Retrieve tooling	0:07:35	0:15:10		x	
4	Install tooling	0:03:57	0:07:54	x		
5	Bend test strip	0:01:48	0:03:36		x	
6	Retrieve material	0:05:00	0:10:00		x	
7	Breaking part	0:01:00	0:02:00	x		
8	Retrieve pallet	0:03:10	0:06:20		x	
9	Breaking part	0:00:57	0:01:54	x		
10	Retrieve vernier calipers	0:00:30	0:01:00			x
11	Breaking part	0:00:38	0:01:16	x		
12	Programming the console	0:05:00	0:10:00		x	
13	Breaking part	0:01:30	0:03:00	x		
14	Adjust NC controller	0:01:20	0:01:20		x	
15	Breaking part	0:00:42	0:00:42	x		
16	Wait for second operator to assist	0:04:45	0:04:45		x	
17	Breaking part	0:00:20	0:00:20	x		
18	Test bend	0:02:11	0:02:11		x	
19	Measure first part	0:00:58	0:00:58	x		
20	Breaking part	0:01:05	0:01:05	x		
	Total			0:19:09	1:08:50	0:01:50
				21.3%	76.6%	2.0%

Figure 26.1   Value Added / Non-Value Added (Before condition)

Before we shared information about the documented improvement with the operator, we asked him if the new layout and new work steps were easier or harder. He expressed a great deal of satisfaction with the new process, describing it as "so much easier than before." He was producing three times as much product, but with much less effort. Kind of like pushing a ship through water with less effort because the barnacles have been scraped off.

Organizational barnacles can grow anywhere. Engineering, order entry, purchasing, finance, and of course, production. Departments may need to be put into "dry-dock" and examined for non-value-added activities.

A fabrication team VA-NVA examination found that 25 percent of its time was spent in non-value added activities. For this $14M company, this meant $3.5 million worth of potential sales opportunity was being left on the table each year.

Interestingly, after a ship has had the barnacles removed, the entire hull must be treated to inhibit the re-growth of barnacles. Similarly, sustainment of improvement in manufacturing environments is by far the most challenging element in the Kaizen process. Changing lifelong behaviors of individuals is necessary to avoid reverting back to non-value-added activities.

Kaizen must become a way of life, and one trip to the dry dock will not create a barnacle free ocean. Continuous improvement is not just a program title, it is a verb; demanding action. Scraping barnacles off a ship is not easy work, but the rewards of improved performance and reduced costs must be worth it, because every viable shipping company in the world does it.

Just as the shipping industry works hard to develop ways of eliminating the growth of barnacles, we must find ways to inhibit the growth of waste in our organizations.

So, where will you start scraping?

Chapter Twenty Seven

Celebrate the Journey

I related this story in my book 'Lean Manufacturing for the Small Shop', but since this is a book of 'chicken soup' type stories, I think that it bears telling again.

I was working at company in the San Francisco area, and as we summarized one visit during a kaizen presentation, we were talking to the team about how much effort is required to sustain the gains. The message I wanted to leave behind was; that if a company wants to become *Lean* they must recognize that it is a *journey* as opposed to a *destination*, and there is a great need to celebrate milestones along the journey.

One of the team members, let's call him Rob, related a story that summarizes how we must approach the journey ahead.

Rob and I had a number of similarities; like me, Rob was approaching middle age, and spreading a little in the middle. Also like me, Rob had at one time been a very fit athlete. Where I played tennis, Rob was a runner. Like me he had also suffered a serious injury that forced him to lead a more sedentary lifestyle for a number of years. The weight started stacking up. He knew that he needed to begin exercising; and soon.

He decided he would start a program of jogging. Running in San Francisco means running either uphill or downhill. Rob's route of choice was a mile long grade beginning at his cul-de-sac and ending at a lone radio and cell phone tower sitting atop a hill behind his neighborhood. A couple hundred yards past the last house in the housing development, the pavement turned to gravel, then as the road turned steeper it became little more than a poorly maintained access road. It was full of pot holes and even washed out in some places. He wondered how radio tower maintenance personnel navigated this goat trail all the way to the top of the hill.

Illustration 27.1   Radio Tower

Every morning for the first few weeks of his new exercise program; Rob would start out by jogging up the steep grade. As he ran, Rob would frequently look uphill at his objective (the radio and cell phone tower).

For the first few days, Rob could only run a short distance before he would have to stop and catch his breath. After dragging himself to the top of the hill, he would walk back home, discouraged that he hadn't been able to run all the way to the top.

After a month, he could often run most of the way, but would always tire before reaching the summit.

Although Rob would have to resort to walking the last few hundred yards, he continued to push himself on.

Each day as he got closer and closer to the radio tower, his lungs would heave to pull in air. The last part of the hill was steeper than the rest. Rob's legs would be burning, screaming for oxygen. Almost to the top...not quite there...he could run no more...he would always finish the climb by walking.

This went on for a few more weeks and Rob just kind of resigned himself to the fact that he would never be able to run all the way to the top without stopping.

Then one morning, Rob took a look outside; preparing for his run. The weather had taken a turn for the wet, as it often does in San Francisco. There was a heavy mist, almost raining, foggy, windy and looked fairly miserable. Rob decided that he would just skip his run for the day.

But just he turned away from the window, he realized; "If I don't go today, I will probably never go again."

So Rob donned his favorite 49'r baseball cap and threw on a windbreaker.

He opened the door tipping his head against the wind and pulled the baseball cap down low over his face to keep the *now* stinging rain out of his eyes, breaking into a jog as he started up the hill.

He thought about the workday ahead as he plodded along. He thought about the weekend. He thought about how the rain would likely be washing leaves into the gutters. He kept running. He promised himself that he would get the ladder out this weekend and clean the gutters.

Then he realized that his ladder was probably buried in the back of his garage. "Man" he thought to himself "the garage needs cleaned and organized so bad. That will take most of a weekend right there."

He realized that his legs were getting tired, but he kept going.

The downpour was letting up a bit and Rob thought about how he ought to take advantage of the rain by spreading some fertilizer on the lawn.

Then, all the sudden, he stopped dead in his tracks.

He looked up, and realized he was at the base of the radio tower.

He had run the entire way and really wasn't even very tired.

Proud of himself, he took off his hat and threw it into the air. He jumped into the air, twisted and celebrated like Sylvester Stallone did as Rocky on the steps of the Philadelphia Art Museum. He ran all the way home excited to tell his wife about his triumph.

The next morning, with spirit renewed from his previous day's success, he jumped from bed to look outside. It was a beautiful clear morning. He dressed and sprang out the door. He took a moment to squint at the former champion, the radio tower, and then confidently broke into a trot.

Rob was surprised at how quickly he seemed to tire. Not like yesterday's victory at all. Half-way up the hill he was running out of steam. And close to the top he had to give up. He stood bent over, hands to knees, gasping for air as he craned his neck to take a disgusted look at the radio tower. Accepting defeat one more time, he turned and dragged himself home; head hung low; spirit broken again.

But not for long.

It took Rob a day or two to figure out what you may already have. The morning that he wore his hat, he was able to negotiate the hill because he was not consumed by a myopic focus of the destination; but rather on the process.

Most mornings, the radio tower seemed so far away. It didn't serve simply as an objective; but because of the distance it also provided a dose of discouragement.

When his mind was totally fixated on getting to the top of the hill, thoughts that could make the journey enjoyable were shoved aside. When he wore the hat, it obstructed the view of the tower and he able to focus on just the *next few steps*; he was able to think about other things.

Rob's success was finally possible because; while he had a clear vision of the objective, it was not constantly overwhelming or as impossible a task since he was free to take his attention off it for periods of time. It no longer required him to focus all his energy on it. Now he was free to *recharge* his mental batteries.

There are similar risks for teams working toward the goal of world class performance that realistically might be one, two, or three years away. It can seem discouraging if they are not allowed to celebrate smaller milestones along the way.

Recognition of progress, however small, is a sign of a well-managed team. Allowing teams to utilize the concept of a model line to implement and practice these techniques on a smaller scale is critical; permitting them to prove to themselves which techniques work in their unique environment.

The teams' success applying these methodologies at a reasonable pace and with clearly defined milestones will have the effect of filling their sails with wind.

I remember driving the family from Oregon to Disneyland years ago. The eighteen hour drive was much too long so celebrate just when we got the magic kingdom. We had to celebrate getting in the van; we celebrated when we crossed the border between Oregon and California. We celebrated again when got to Sacramento, realizing that we were half way.

We had to find new and creative ways to celebrate as we motored along Interstate Five for another five hundred miles.

The journey to world class performance will probably take longer than you would like it to. Don't permit discouragement and impatience to minimize the value of the journey itself. One major benefit of the transformation process is seeing each other grow as individuals. Celebrate that; and the rest of the journey.

Chapter Twenty Eight

People are like Bamboo

Years ago I read a book called HEROZ. It was a bit of a fairy tale about a castle protected by archers. The story was really about the manufacturing of *arrows*, supplying them to those responsible to slay dragons (problems) that attacked the castle (company). Having a quiver full of *arrows* (skills) to solve problems is key for any manager. That what *this* book, and *this* story is about; trying to provide you with *arrows* to fill your *quiver*.

I was visiting my sister prior to a family barbeque. She was planting bamboo around her fish pond. I guess it would be more accurate to say she was transplanting bamboo shoots around her fish pond. All the bamboo had come from a local nursery.

My sister is a master gardener, so I asked her why she was planting foot tall bamboo shoots instead of growing them from seeds. She had a green house full of other plants she grew from seeds and sold to others, it just seemed curious to me that she would pay someone else to grow these *bamboo seedlings*.

It just so happened that at the time, I was working with a client who had a number of extremely resistant team members. The message in this story is this; as you lead teams of people situations will arise where you need to coach them to move from a place where they are comfortable to a place where they need to go.

Sports team coaches do it all the time. If you can; imagine for a moment being the coach in a locker room at half time, seeing your basketball team down by twenty points to a less capable rival team.

What could you say to motivate them to achieve the performance that you know they are capable of? The coach has to look everywhere for ideas, inspiration, illustrations. If he or she doesn't have a *quiver* full of *arrows* there's little hope that the coach will have ammunition to rely on when the team needs a mind altering story to infuse them with confidence, energy and excitement.

It's the same with work teams, you can never predict when you will run headlong into a team who may have given up; are uninspired, unproductive, or are unwilling to deliver the extra effort needed.

From where will the inspiration you need to communicate originate? I've learned that you have to keep your eyes open all the time. Keep a journal if you have to. Observe everyone and everything; ask yourself if there is a story there; a story that you can turn into an *arrow*; a future coaching opportunity you can add to your quiver.

As I mentioned before, I asked my sister why she bought bamboo shoots instead of planting them from seeds. She said that it takes a very long time to plant and grow bamboo from seed, and she wanted bamboo around her fish pond right away.

Illustration 28.1 Bamboo   Source: Bamboo Revolution

Having visited Japan, and seeing lots of bamboo growing everywhere like weeds I asked her to explain.

"Well" she said "you are right about bamboo once it is established. When we plant bamboo, we often cut a 55 gallon barrel and bury it in the ground as a container; otherwise the bamboo will grow under my neighbor's fence there..." She pointed to her neighbor's yard. "...and take over his yard." "But growing it from seed is another matter. Let's say I want to plant bamboo here. If I till the soil, pull out the sod, fill in fresh top soil, plant bamboo seeds, and then fertilize the soil, water and watch all this year I won't see any bamboo growing." I nodded, and she continued "Next year there would probably be weeds growing in here where I planted the bamboo, so I'd have to carefully pull them out so as not to uproot the germinating bamboo. But I wouldn't have any bamboo to show for my efforts the entire second growing season either." My eyes were wide open with anticipation now. "Third year...nothing!" She paused. "Fourth year? Nothing."

Now I was starting to wonder why anyone would want to try growing bamboo. She let me think about it for a few seconds as she drove the hand held shovel into the dirt and implanted another bamboo shoot.

"The fifth year is different." She said "Some species of bamboo can shoot up four feet in one day; eighty feet in one season!" I was blown away. What a story.

If that's as far as it went, then I had a nice piece of trivia to relate at the next barbeque I attended. But I saw this as another *arrow* that I could add to my quiver.

I realized that people and bamboo are a lot alike. We do not always recognize the kind of growth we want or need, or that we would like to see from our teams. But, we cannot short cut the process.

In growing bamboo, I am sure that you could apply a heat lamp or other device to help speed up the germination process. But too much heat and you would kill the growth. So it is with people. You plant the seeds (the ideas), and then you have to wait for the ideas to germinate.

It takes longer than you would like, but if you assume no growth is happening, you might try short cutting the process, or worse yet; give up and figuratively *till* under the current initiative and accompanying efforts, try (planting) some other initiative (some new program), killing the freshly germinated ideas in the process.

We've all seen the folly of companies who get into a costly *book of the month routine*. They move from one initiative to another without allowing adequate time for their teams to adjust to the new direction before abandoning it for the *latest* business fad. They rarely see any benefit, and the stress of such an approach damages the growth process and willingness of teams to try anything new.

You have to look for the growth. "Peel the dirt back" so to speak, look into the soil and see if you can recognize growth. It may be small at first, but if you acknowledge people for getting it right, they will seek that recognition again. *Catch the Eagle in flight* is a phrase that means you need to seek opportunities to catch people doing it right.

People and bamboo are more alike than we think. Patience is required. Just planting the seeds is not enough. With bamboo you have to go back and nurture the seedlings, pull out competing weeds, water, fertilize and feed the young plants. Teams and individuals are even more complex. In order to coach them to their full potential you will need even more patience.

And an occasional story.

Chapter Twenty Nine

Quick kills

One of the most interesting aspects of conducting a kaizen event is seeing the dozens if not hundreds of ideas often generated by the team. Besides major changes like new plant layouts or work assignments, the team collects many small ideas often referred to as quick kills (because we are quickly killing a problem for someone).

Giving individuals on the team a goal of generating at least three ideas per day helps them *key in* and validate comments and concerns from the people being observed during the value stream mapping process.

It's not usually an earth shattering idea. More often, it's a simple fix; a $25.00 investment that makes someone's life easier, in the process makes them more productive and maybe most important of all; happier.

One example that comes to mind is from a secondary wood manufacturing firm. Because most of the old growth timber is long gone, when they find a beautiful piece of wood in a tree; one without defects like pitch pockets or knots, they try to extract the most value from it as possible.

Rather than milling the pristine piece of wood into a single component, they slice the block into multiple veneers; like slicing individual pieces out of a block of cheese. Once the veneer is sliced, they finger-joint or butt-joint the veneer end to end, and then coil it up onto a 2000 ft. roll (about 3 feet in diameter)

Because these blocks of wood all vary slightly in width, the freshly sliced veneers must be machined to a uniform width prior to joining and rolling them together.

Our kaizen team was observing the process of machining these small stacks (fliches) of veneer. The operator would take a stack about four inches thick (about two boards worth of veneer) and run them through a moulder and then tape them together at both ends before transferring them to the finger joint machine operator.

After each flitch was moulded, he would pick up a roll of tape and dig for the end of the tape, peel off two feet of tape and then wrap it around the end before moving to the other end of the flich, repeating the process.

Someone on the kaizen team suggested getting him a tape dispenser for each end of the table he was working on. Total price: $30.

Illustration 29.1 Tape Dispenser

197

We calculated that it would save him an average of 3 seconds per end, 6 seconds per flitch, at 400 flitches per day and 250 days per year a little over 80 hours per year labor savings. About $1000. Not a bad payback. Items like this are not going to make or break a company. But think about it this way. In order to put $1,000 on the bottom line, a company that operates with a 25% gross margin must sell $4,000 worth of product.

At the same company our team noticed that a lady who put weather stripping into exterior door frames had to cut weather stripping by hand whenever the door was a custom size. Weather stripping for standard door sizes were factory cut by their supplier. But when the door was extra tall, narrow or wider than usual she would have to get out a razor knife, protractor and tape measure, pull out the weather stripping from a thousand foot roll; measure and miter cut three pieces (45 degree angles on each end of the header, a square cut and 45 degree angle on one end of each of the door frame legs).

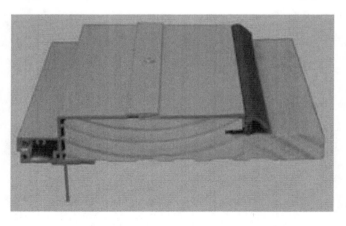

Illustration 29.2 Door frame example w/weather striping   Source: JJJspecialty.com

A kaizen team member suggested routing a slight groove into her work table, imbedding a tape measure into the groove (so it was just below the surface) and attaching a paper cutter (permanently fixed at a 45 degree angle) at one end of her table.

This saved her about one minute of effort per door frame. Since it only applied to special door frames (about 5% of their business) it didn't have huge financial impact, but it only cost about $125, and her working life got better. At 5% of 40,000 door frames per year, it reduced labor by 2,000 minutes per year (about 33 hours). This translated into a three month payback. But more importantly in this case, morale and safety was definitely improved.

Many times, the improvements made are not going to show up immediately on the bottom line. But what is the value of happier employees? What is the value of a safer work environment? What is the value of a higher quality product? What is the value of reduced scrap?

We always ask our kaizen teams to consider how to make the persons working life more enriching, safer, more fun. I ask questions like this: "How would you set this up for your Mother?" I can tell you that I would make my mom's life as easy as I could possibly make it. I would not design a work space that required my mom to reach far over her head multiple times per day, or bend to the floor over and over. I would do my utmost to ensure that my mom's work area was safe and ergonomically comfortable.

In the process of making the person's work easier and safer, you make generally make them more productive as well.

Chapter Thirty

Supporting Their Habit

In the high desert of Central Oregon there is a family owned business that makes products for the trucking industry among others. They make a product that physically moves the floor of the truck bed back and forth so that forklifts are not necessary to unload the cargo.

Trucking companies that employ this product avoid the process of tipping the entire trailer when unloading bark chips, sawdust, potatoes, trash and other materials. As you can imagine, this provides trucking customers a major cost reduction in material handling equipment and maintenance along with enormous improvements in safety.

I was engaged to assist with a set-up reduction event in 2004 and since then have worked with this terrific company off and on, right up to the writing of this text.

Illustration 30.1 Three Sisters Source: City-Data.com

I will always remember the first team I worked with there. It surprised me a little that when we took the team photograph they balked at the suggestion to take the picture with them standing beside their machines or in front of the company sign. Instead they wanted me to snap their picture with the Three Sister's Mountain range behind them.

I came to appreciate that while these men worked as machinists; that was not their passion. They worked at this company to support their habit. They were farmers and ranchers; a vocation that is not likely to make them rich or for that matter, even pay the bills. After ten hours of running a lathe or mill, these men would go home and drive a tractor or tend to their animals until well past nightfall. They loved the land and that was their main topic of conversation whenever we would take a break. While they were interested in the set-up reduction event and how it might make their company and therefore their jobs more sustainable, you could just tell that their hearts were really back home with their worn out farm implements and concerns about water rights, rainfall, fertilizer and the upcoming calving season.

I introduce you to these four men because I want you to know that these are not rich men. If they were rich, I am one hundred percent convinced that they would not have been working in the machine shop of this company, but rather they would have been working the soil and spending time with their horses, cattle, sheep or other animals.

The fact that they were not rich men will be important at the end of this story.

We focused on two different machines (a mill and a lathe) with the initial objective to reduce set-up time by 50%.

Our observations were about the same for each machine. Just about two and a half hours per set-up. The machinist traveled just over 2,000 feet; necessitated by the need to retrieve tools from a common tool room.

The kaizen team came up with about twenty recommendations including the application of what the Japanese refer to as a "water-spider" or Misu-shu-mashi. Like a water bug dancing across the top of a pond, there are people in the Japanese manufacturing plants who don't really have a job description; rather they *dance* around wherever they are needed to ensure that the *flow* of material or information is maintained. The team saw the possibility for one person to take on a more meaningful role regarding tool room management and tool delivery (to machinists). They estimated that one person could help keep the machinists (17 mills and 10 lathes) at their machines instead of walking around the shop looking for tooling, materials, paperwork or other items during set-ups.

This water spider could not be *'Jo Ordinary'* off the street. He or she would have to be an experienced operator understanding the unique needs of the products, materials, machines and company routing procedures. It meant that they would probably have to take one of their best operators off a machine and put him or her in this new assignment. There would be significant cost associated with such a responsible position.

Recommendation	Cost
Assign one person dedicated to set-up (water spider) activity	$31,200
Area defined to do this (i.e: computer, racks, tables, carts)	$500
Coded tools (defined system)	$0
Programming to begin using standard tool geometry etc...	$0
Common language	$0
Team approach (machinists set-up)	$0
Tool carts	$500
Tool setter	$15,000
Additionally misc. tool holders	$25,000
Buy Griffo Bros. Soft ware	$1,300
Equally distribute t nuts for each set-up	$0
Modify the optical comparitor for use as a set-up tool	$1,500
5-S Boards	$1,100
Better identify material and due date in baskets (plastic W/O card?)	$0
Permanently mark tool holders (for dedicated tool kits)	$0
Eliminate screw downs (on Mill) use ball locks	$8,000
More collets	$5,000
Perform a tool inventory	$0
Air wrenches at each machine	$3,000
Bore gauges and thread gauges (set for mills / lathes)	$5,000
Tooling cabinets (waterloo) $1500 * 4	$6,000
Forklift just for the machine shop	$0
Total investment	$103,100
Total savings	$733,179
ROI	1.7

Figure 30.1 Team recommendations with costs and benefits

We tried an experiment (simulation) of their ideas and in both cases recognized a 92% reduction in machine downtime.

Conservatively, the team calculated this improvement would translate into a $733,000 annual savings.

The cost of implementing all of their ideas would be just over $103,000 the first year (the labor cost of the water-spider position was the only repeating expenditure). I am always amazed at the results of teams like this but this seemed hard to believe even for me. So I was more than a little concerned that

203

they were over estimating the return on investment. I tested them by asking them a couple of questions: "How confident are you that we have a new process that can be applied generically to all machines and all products?" I didn't let them answer yet, but asked a few follow-up questions "What if management says no? What if they will not invest the $103,000? Would you invest your money in this idea if they would let you have the potential profit (knowing it is only potential at this point)?"

They looked at each other and in unison said "Yes!" One of the team members summed up their feelings on the matter "I would invest my own money in this project, because I know this will work!"

"Good enough for me!" I said. Knowing that these were not rich men; certainly not inclined to squander limited resources on a half baked idea. I was confident that they were committed. "Then let's take this recommendation to management!"

Of course their management team did adopt their recommendations and I know that they recognized the return on investment because that project was conducted in the fall of 2004 and they had me back in 2006 to facilitate a similar event in another department of the company.

As the writing of this book we continue to work with this organization including the development of a complete plant layout; cellularizing their entire facility into value streams. I am convinced that the company would not be utilizing our services had they not recognized the projected financial benefits from these earlier projects.

Chapter Thirty One

It's not always what you think

I was invited to visit a company in Colorado a few years back. They specialized in fabricating custom stainless steel kitchen equipment for hotel and casino restaurants; buffets and hospital equipment. Their lead time through engineering and the fabrication shop was about three weeks.

Illustration 31.1 Stainless steel kitchen equipment

If you know anything about commercial building schedules you know that timelines are always changing, and since the kitchen equipment is one of the last items to be installed, final dimensions are often unknown until the last minute. Shelving and food preparation tables must fit in areas where variations in the sheetrock process can change dimensions of a room right up until the day of installation. You can imagine why they needed help.

Their engineering department was struggling to provide accurate and timely part manufacturing drawings to the shop.

As I toured the plant I paid close attention to the manufacturing processes and came to realize that their main problem was not related to the shop, but rather was the result of a cumbersome design and drafting process.

When I expressed my concern, the General Manager assured me that they had a plan to relieve the bottleneck in engineering. They were about to hire an additional engineer and two more draftspersons. This would require three additional 'seats' of Autocad (drafting software licenses) and expansion of the engineering department.

I suggested that they consider postponing hiring additional engineering staff until we were able to perform a kaizen event in that department.

We discovered that based on average $6MM in annual sales, the engineering department needed to be producing $120,000 of engineered drawing to the shop every week. They were producing about $80,000. Not only that, but the accuracy of the drawings produced was far less than desired.

In my initial tour I saw a laser operator furiously key-stroking a calculator as a full sheet of stainless steel sat motionless on the laser table. When I question him about it he said that "Each engineer uses a different bend deduction formula. I need to verify the figures before I feel comfortable cutting an entire sheet of expensive material, only to find out later that the program was in error."

The DPMO (defects per million opportunities) output from engineering, (a six sigma quality measurement) was over 30,000. This required redundant checking throughout the manufacturing process; slowing down delivery to the customer. This was in addition to the initial delays in getting slow moving shop prints delivered to production.

During a three day kaizen event, we value stream mapped the engineering process, realigned the standard work (assignments of *who* does *what*). We calculated an engineering takt time based on the $120,000 weekly demand, and developed a pull system that ensured drawings continued to flow rather than spending time piled on someone's desk.

In the *after* condition, the same team, with the same number of workstations, utilizing the same space was able to consistently produce $132,000 (an improvement of over 35%) all while reducing their DPMO by over 50%.

Developing best practices, standardizing engineering processes, print nomenclature and layout not only sped up engineering but provided the shop a consistent form of information; making their work easier and more uniform.

Sometimes companies look at the term 'Lean Manufacturing' and assume that it applies only to the shop. These processes work as well in administrative (and even in service organizations) as well as they do in manufacturing environments.

Chapter Thirty Two

Get close to your customer

Some of these stories are warnings. This is one such example.

I always have to manage a delicate balancing act when meeting new client management teams.   They often know just enough about lean manufacturing to be dangerous.   The old saying is "They don't know what they don't know."

I have to be careful to not come across as dogmatic or prescriptive as we map out the strategic plan. I never want to be like the consultant who made a manager stand in the middle of the plant with a sign around his neck which read "OBSTACLE" just because he had the *audacity* to challenge the approach.

As bizarre at that sounds, it is just one of the horror stories I've heard about some of the *old school* consultants who came directly from Japan.   That approach may have worked just fine in a different culture, but does little to reshape the thinking or foster *buy-in* of people here on the American continent.

So when one client insisted that our first project be in the electronics assembly area of their plant (this process was in the middle of the value stream), I did my best to strongly suggest a different approach while not driving a wedge between myself and the team.

I tactfully explained that if you start in the middle of the process, sometimes you make improvements and the product now hurries through the improved system only to wait longer.

The downstream processes are not improved, so the customer doesn't see any improvement in lead time reduction. The improvement is hidden by the now *sub-optimized* value stream. You can optimize one process and actually sub-optimize the overall process.

My efforts to tactfully move them toward the end of the process *closer to the customer* fell on deaf ears. As an invited guest I am not always at liberty to make more than a recommendation. To walk away in disgust and turn down the project would only serve to prolong the waste, so in this case I took the project fully knowing that the first phase was probably not going to have a marked reduction in lead-time.

The kaizen team did have a remarkable result. Rebalancing the electronic assembly reduced wait time in final assembly and reduced labor cost by a significant amount. Yet as foretold during our strategic planning session; lead-time to the customer remained largely unaffected.

The next project changed all that. This time the steering team decided to take my advice and start in final assembly. In doing so we trimmed off days of lead time. After moving upstream one process at a time, the company recognized nearly a 50% reduction in lead time. One of the products this company manufactures is equipment used to grind, reclaim and recycle material from buildings being demolished.

It just so happened that we finished the lean transformation project at this client company just about the same time hurricane Katrina hit the gulf coast.

Illustration 32.1 Home demolition

Suddenly there was an enormous need for recycling equipment like theirs. They saw a 30% increase in demand, and because of the work done during the previous year; they were able to absorb the additional work without any significant hiring or overtime.

They have experienced an 80% reduction in inventory, 50% reduction in lead time, 50% improvement in quality and better space utilization.

While they may have eventually had a similar result moving from work center to work center with kaizen events based on evidence of excess waste, it would have likely taken years instead of months. I am sure that they would not have been in the same position to react to the Katrina effect if they had not gotten *close to their customer*, by moving from final assembly upstream.

Chapter Thirty Three

Hoshin Kanri

When my wife and I found out that we were going to have a baby I decided take a break from consulting, getting off the road for a while.

I took a full time job with a manufacturer of secondary wood products (see the story Tool Room Transformed) for customers like Pella Windows, Anderson doors among others.

The owner was extremely intelligent (IQ approaching 170) and was part of the Mensa organization (an international group of people made up of those with exceptionally high intelligence).

Yet after working for this man of incredible intellect for two years he suddenly died of a massive stroke. He left behind a $65MM business now being run by five vice presidents (VP of Operations, VP of Sales, VP of Material Procurement, VP of R&D, and VP of Finance). As smart as the owner was, he was somehow unable to transmit his vision into the minds of these five company leaders. Therefore after his passing each Vice President seemed to be directed by a different compass.

Back to this story in a minute.

During the Japanese attack on the United States at Pearl Harbor the Japanese naval fleet had to navigate thousands of miles of ocean. They had to moving together as one silent unit.

Each Ship Commander had to move his ship and supplies during the day, at night, through storms, rough seas and unforeseen conditions; all without the luxury of radio communication. The flotilla included aircraft carriers, destroyers, fueling ships, support vessels; each with unique needs and challenges.

Illustration 33.1 Japanese Naval Fleet   Source: Google images

Having operated a small boat, I can tell you it is hard enough to navigate even on your own. But these sailors somehow had to negotiate the expansive Pacific Ocean; staying together on course, avoiding collisions between each other and choreographing their movements in an effort to remain hidden.

They used a system called Hoshin Kanri. A methodology for each ship's captain (and every sailor) to make decisions in keeping with the team's overall objective, all without the benefit of continual communication. Without a clear vision, objective and game plan in every captain's mind there would surely have been collisions.

Back to our story; regardless of the fact that my boss had all the leaders in our company read "Lean Thinking" (by Womack and Jones) somehow; before his passing he was unable to implant his vision (his objective) into the minds of the five Vice Presidents.

It was like; after his passing there was a collective sigh of relief from the five Vice Presidents. As if to say; "Whew, well at least we don't have to think about that lean stuff anymore." Their hearts just were not in it.

Illustration 33.2   Compass   Source: Google images

I stayed on for another few months, but the ensuing confusion and conflict of five people holding five separate compasses each with a different heading seemed to be destined for an eventual collision and potential sinking of the organization.

No one could have predicted the owner's passing. In hindsight I see now that I might have applied greater effort in helping him to communicate his vision.

Live and learn. We always think that there will be time. We can't be sure of that. Make every day count. Take the necessary steps *now* to communicate your vision. You can't assume that people will get it by osmosis.

Chapter Thirty Four

Keep it Simple

One of the fundamental techniques in the lean manufacturing tool box is TPM (Total Productive maintenance). It is easy to hide machine reliability issues when companies are departmentalized. If one machine *goes down* due to a breakdown or lack of maintenance you can usually have the department work overtime or change peoples' schedules to make up for a short term capacity constraint.

When companies cellularlize, there may be only one key machine in each cell, so when it goes down the entire cell is down. This puts customer deliveries at risk.

So over the years companies on the world class path have developed numerous maintenance programs to ensure that key equipment is always available when needed.

There is a technique called OEE (overall equipment effectiveness) which is a mathematical calculation of uptime percentage.

For example; if a machine is available for eight (8) hours per day, that translates to 480 minutes. If the operator shuts the machine down for two-10 minute breaks each day, then 20 minutes of downtime must be subtracted from the original 480; resulting in only 460 minutes or 95.8% of available uptime.

If machine set-ups require 30 minutes per day of additional downtime then the remaining 430 minutes results in an 89.5%

effective uptime. Downtime due to loading and unloading material, fault time or other causes may result in even lower equipment effectiveness.

Calculating OEE (Overall Equipment Effectiveness)

Equipment Availability		Value	Units	
A	Total Shift Time	480	min	
B	Planned Downtime	20	min	
C	Net Available Time	460	min	A-B
Non-Value Added Time				
D	Set-Ups & Adjustments	30	min	
E	Fault Time	15	min	
F	Idle In + Idle Out Time	30	min	
G	Total Downtime	75	min	D+E+F
H	Total Uptime	385	min	C-G
I	Equipment Availabilty	84%		H/C
Performance Efficiency				
J	Total Parts Run	400	parts	
K	Average Cycle Time	50	sec/part	
L	Performance Efficiency	87%		(K*J/60)/H
Quality Rate				
M	Total Rejects/Defective Parts	50	parts	
N	Quality Rate	88%		(J-M)/J
Overall Equipment Effectiveness:		63%		I*L*N

Figure 34.1   OEE (Overall Equipment Effectiveness) Calculator

If you would like to obtain a copy of the OEE calculator shown here, please visit our website to request a copy.

Working with one client, they had old equipment without CNC (computer numeric control) devices, and it was hard to measure the true machine uptime.

A very creative maintenance manager found a simple solution to measure the OEE of these antique machines. He went to the local hardware store and bought some electric alarm clocks.

He wired the alarm clocks directly into each machines drive motor. Whenever the machine was running, so was the clock. We had the operator re-set the clock to 12:00 each morning. At the end of the day we were surprised to find that the machine was actually running less than four hours per day.

Illustration 34.1 Alarm Clock   Source: Google images

The operators were confident that the machine was running well over 70%; but the alarm clock showed that it was in actuality running less than 50%; a simple, yet profound method of visualizing machine effectiveness.

Another example of simplicity came from a client in Long Beach California. Each machine was outfitted with a pair of side by side time card slots.

Thirty slots each containing a simple laminated card represented the maintenance tasks required for each day of the month. On the first day of the month the first card is removed by the operator and instructions followed regarding oiling, greasing, inspecting and cleaning..

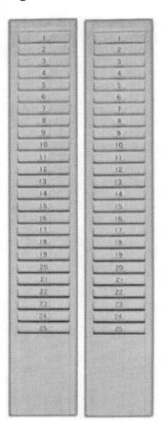

Illustration 34.2 Time card slots   Source: Google images

Once the required tasks were completed for the day, the card was placed in the second card holding device. Anyone could walk by at any time, and see which cards had been moved, leaving no question about the machine's maintenance status.

This inspecting through cleaning process puts the operator more in control of his or her machine

Imagine a racecar driver coming back into the pits after a test run. The driver takes a participative role in the car's performance. He or she doesn't just jump out of the car and walk off; rather, they interact with the crew chief to share their observations.

After all, they are the ones spending the majority of the time operating the vehicle (machine) they are in the best position to share information with the maintenance team.

It is the same with manufacturing teams; by being in tune with the machine they operate, they are in a unique position to offer their maintenance teams important observations much like a racecar driver might: "I felt a vibration that wasn't there before." or "I smelled something like a belt burning." or "It sounds different today." or "This guide rail seems rough to the touch." Using all their senses, they are able to truly contribute to the care and maintenance of the equipment rather than just being a passive operator. That is what the word *total* in the term Total Productive Maintenance means; *total* involvement.

I remember visiting a company in Little Rock, Arkansas. They rebuilt railcar bearings. Tearing these huge bearings apart, cleaning and polishing them was a dirty job; requiring huge machines.

As the General Manager walked me through the dark dreary building everything suddenly stopped and all the exterior doors simultaneously flew open and the sunlight from outside exploded into the 30,000 square foot building. A horn blew and the thirty or so employees all streamed quickly to the exits.

I frantically looked around and then at my host, thinking "this must be a fire drill." He must have seen the worry in my eyes, he said "No problem; the machine just broke down over there; happens all the time." He moved me along on the tour, and the maintenance crew soon wheeled up in a golf cart.

But I was still looking back at all the employees who were by now all outside enjoying a smoke break.

After our tour I mentioned to the Manager that having the machine go down was almost like a mini-vacation; a reward system. We decided to try something different. Next time the machine broke we would have the team stay inside with the maintenance team; watching the repair and listening to the mechanics problem solve the issue. This would give the operators a chance to become familiar with cause and effect information that could help them bring concerns to the attention of the maintenance crew long before an actual machine breakdown occurred.

Chapter Thirty Five

Finding the Common Denominator

Of major concern in most job shops is the task of identifying a meaningful rate of production. Few of my clients have the luxury of making the same product day after day, so instead of determining the number of pieces shipped, they must determine how many *units of work* are being demanded in order to accurately calculate how often they need to produce a work unit.

When your product is not the same each day (like it might be at Toyota for example) you must find something about your product line that is uniform; a common unit of measure that everyone can understand and which allows the application of Takt Time (a mathematical equation that allows you to set and maintain a manufacturing rhythm). For lack of a better term what these companies need is a common denominator.

I was invited to Edmonton Alberta Canada to work with a manufacturer of oil pipeline equipment. They had already worked with another consultant and had just about given up because the consultant had insisted that the application of the Toyota Production System T.O.P. (takt time, one piece flow, and pull systems) was inflexible. Despite their diverse product mix they were told that they must apply these tools exactly as Toyota had or else the consultant would not be willing to help them. They had tried but eventually threw their arms up in defeat because the methodology just didn't seem to work in their high mix, low volume environment.

When I joined them they had just been informed by a new plant manager to give Lean another chance.

You could have cut the skepticism with a knife.

We selected a smaller value stream (about 20% of their business) in which they manufactured large pipe fittings. This segment of the business produced about 7,000 pieces of pipe each year.

Because of the seasonality of the industry, they must produce the majority of the product (5,000) during the six months winter period (when the perma-frost allows their oil drilling customers to perform work on the tundra).

Utilizing the lean manufacturing principles requires that everything be determined by takt time.

For example; to determine the number of machines needed, you must divide the machine cycle time by takt time. To determine the number of operators needed, you divide operator cycle time by takt time. To determine a lot size or kanban (replenishment point) signal, you must divide the time it will take to manufacture or order and receive more material by takt time.

Takt time is determined by dividing available time by demand, thus they have a two season takt time. They have roughly 1000 hours (6 months, assuming one shift) in each season.

For example: 1,000 hours divided by 2,000 units means they will need to produce one unit every 30 minutes during the summer months. Every 12 minutes for the 5000 units required during the winter season.

But for this company it was a little more complicated. They also had variations in the complexity of each unit. And that's why they had initially struggled. While they would indeed make 7,000 units per year, these units varied significantly in shape, weight and size.

When we studied their PQ (product-quantity) data we found that there were actually three primary product categories. We determined that a single flange pipe (shown as part "A"), would be used as their common denominator. Therefore ten units like this would be equal to ten units of work.

Part A – 2000 per year - 1 work unit

Part B – 2500 per year – 1.6 work units

Part C – 2500 per year – 2.1 work units

Illustration 35.1   Variations in types of pipe

They determined that a product which has a second flange on the opposite end (part "B") did not require twice as much work, but initial time studies showed that it required about 1.6 (160%) as much effort and time to produce as type "A" parts. Therefore, 10 physical units of type B parts would be assigned 16 work units.

A third category of parts (part "C") included a smaller, perpendicular flange on the pipe. This variation required 2.1 (210%) as much effort as a type "A" single flange pipe.

If they simply divide the 7,000 annual demand into the annual available time of 2,000 hours, their takt time would be .286 hours (17 minutes) per unit. This provided a false indicator however, since they would always seem to be behind while producing type "C" parts.

In order to calculate a meaningful takt time, they must use a weighted average for the current demand of all pipe variations that they manufacture.

For example, let's say they sell 2,000 part A's, and 2,500 each of part types B and C. Multiplying each quantity against the level of complexity provides a clearer picture of how much work is ahead of them in the coming year.

2,000 x 1   = 2,000

2,500 x 1.6   = 4,000

2,500 x 2.1   = 5,250

Total   = 11,250   (units of units)

The total weighted average work units produced every year is 11,250. By dividing this number into the 2,000 hours (120,000 minutes) available per year, the resulting value .178 reflects the manufacturing rhythm or takt time, in this case .178 or 17.8% of an hour (10.67 minutes) per unit.

But we can't forget about the seasonality. During the slow summer months, they should produce the 2,000 unit demand (3,214 work units) at a takt time of .31 hours (18.7 minutes) per unit. During the winter, the takt time for the remaining 5,000 units should be produced at a hybrid takt time of .12 hours (7.5 minutes) per unit.

Of course when they produce a type "C" product they will get 2.1 credits on their hour-by-hour chart.

Now they have a meaningful takt time; one that can be updated if the sales percentage ever changes.

It is common to have two or three takt times. Kind of like a three speed transmission. Any minor fluctuation in demand can be managed by adding or subtracting an hour or two per week, or a day or two per month. Takt time should not be changed very often, only when there is a *substantial and sustained* change in demand.

Applying lean at an OEM like Toyota, Harley Davidson or John Deere is easy compared to adopting the techniques at a job shop. You just have to be willing to be more creative. Happily this client did not give up, even after an initial and major setback.

Chapter Thirty Six

What we give up when we become a manager

I was new to consulting. Not very polished, that's for sure. One of my first jobs was in New England. Travel was still romantic and I was having a ball.

My first trip to a new client just south of Boston meant that I had to travel from the West Coast on a Sunday. Getting in a day early provided me a chance to stop and see Plymouth Rock, and other historical sites that I had only read about.

I was used to working for a company where people were respected, ideas were explored, employees felt enfranchised and managers were well trained to interact with each other and with the people they managed.

The company I was contracted to work with in New England had been started eighteen years earlier by a guy right out of high school. He had been growing his business for nearly two decades, and despite little or no business training had built it into a $5MM business employing about thirty people.

This family owned shop supplied precision sheet metal parts to AT&T; as did many companies in the New England area; a mom and pop shop which had started out in a garage, and had now grown up into a medium sized shop.

The owner realized that they needed to adopt world class manufacturing practices. He tended to hire young people, most right out of high school. He said that he liked hiring young people because they had not had time to develop bad work habits; they were still impressionable blank slates that he could develop into uniform team members. I showed up having never met the owner in person. Our first contract had been negotiated over the phone.

Monday morning I met with the set-up reduction team at 7:00 AM, and after a short training session, we hit the shop floor to begin our project. About 8:00 AM I noticed that the team seemed distracted, and I happened to catch a couple of them glancing toward the door leading from the shop to the office. Precisely at 8:00 AM the owner of the company (let's call him Rich) burst through the door, laughing and slapping everyone on the back with a hearty "Good mornin!' " His good mood was infectious, and everyone in the shop adopted his high energy, effervescent attitude. I thought to myself "This is going to be a great gig!"

The next day I again met with the team at 7:00 AM and we continued our work in the shop. Again, at a few minutes until 8:00 AM I noticed that the team seemed distracted. And as with the previous morning, I noticed that some of them seemed unduly interested in the door leading to the office. On this day Rich came through the door just a few minutes after 8:00 AM. No cheery "Good mornin" this time. No slaps on the back or energetic walk through the shop. Today Rich seemed morose, depressed, nearly dragging his knuckles on the ground. In fact he seemed like he didn't want to interact with people and was *short* with those who did approach him with questions about projects they were working on.

I couldn't help but notice that again, the entire shop adopted Rich's demeanor. But this time instead of high energy all day, everyone was morose and depressed all day.

I don't know if Rich had had an argument with his wife that morning, or has gotten a ticket on the way to work or whatever; but after those first two days, I started paying attention to the dynamic that seemed to play out each morning at 8:00 AM; Rich's arrival, and everyone else's attitude alignment to his mood-de-jour.

On Thursday of that first week Rich invited me out to dinner. Even though the kaizen team was going to make a formal presentation on Friday, he wanted an update. He asked "How is the team doing?"

I filled him in on the progress of the team and confirmed that the team was having a very successful project and that he would be very impressed with the results.

Then he asked "How am I doing?"

I paused, (remember I was new to consulting, unpolished and not a lot of experience at coaching the owner of a multi-million dollar business). I said something like: "Rich…I think you either need to care about people…or you ought to hire someone who does."

Illustration 36.1 Name plaque   Source: Google images

He didn't even try to hide his shock. He sat bolt upright in the restaurant booth for what seemed a lifetime, but was probably more like five seconds. Then he asked me to explain myself.

I said "I have always been taught that when we take on the role of leader we give up the right to have a bad day. When we come in and impose our mood on the young people who work for us, treating them with less respect than we did the day before, just because we are having a bad day, they go home with their self esteem less intact than when they arrived. We do not have the moral right to do that to another person." I paused, just in case he wanted to interject a comment.

He was listening intently, so I continued, "Studies have shown that for every negative comment made to a person it takes seventeen positive reinforcements to equalize the effect of that negativity. That is very expensive. Stephen Covey refers to that as the emotional bank account. If we were to overdraw a literal bank account and they charged us 17 to 1 for every dollar we overdrew, we would quickly realize it is too expensive. We need to have that same sensitivity toward the emotional bank accounts of those we manage."

He sat for a few moments and then said "Thank you"

I don't know if Rich ever really *got it*.

Even though there was much more work I could have done there, I was never invited back. I hope I did not damage Rich's self esteem, I likely would have approached that situation differently now (16 years later), but it was a message that he needed to hear, even if it was probably hard to hear.

229

I hope that he took the message to heart. I hope we all do.

I often get asked by managers "Why can't I get my people excited? I send them to seminars, I bring in trainers, and we give them books and watch videos and even take tours of other companies."

Illustration 36.2 Empty gas gauge   Source: Google images

I usually ask them a couple of questions like; "When was the last time you had to worry about whether or not you had enough gas to get to work?   Or, when was the last time you had to worry about putting milk on the table for your kids' breakfast? Or agonized about how you were going to take care of your aging parents? Or paying your electric bill at home?"

Everyone wishes they had more, that's just human nature. But when the day-to-day financial reality and stresses of an hourly worker is compared to their managers' there is usually no comparison. So when we try to get our teams excited about making the company more profitable and there is no substantial change in their personal financial position, their focus or excitement is not likely going to be about improving the company's bottom line. They are more likely going to be consumed with how they are going to scrape enough pocket change together to avoid having their car run out of gas on their way home.

This is not to say we have to give up, or bribe them into participating. Human emotion is a powerful motivator, and I would never suggest manipulation as a vehicle for getting engagement. However, when someone takes a sincere interest in us we are motivated to reciprocate.

If you do not really don't care about the people who you work with (or that work for you) don't pretend that you do; they will see insincerity from a mile away.

If the struggles they face are unimportant to you, then the struggles you face as the manager of a company, division, department or team will be less than important to them.

If we are honest with ourselves we will recognize that we can't do this without them, it behooves us to let them know that we are aware of that fact. Ask for their help. You need them.

It has been said that it is physiologically impossible for a human to deny a cry for help. That means that physically, emotionally even spiritually it is nearly impossible for us to turn our back and ignore someone who is sincerely begging for our assistance.

I live in Newport, Oregon; I often walk along the fishing dock. Imagine that one day as I take my walk among the many boats moored along the dock I hear a cry for help.

Someone has fallen off their boat and is struggling to reach the dock. It is impossible for me to turn away and walk off saying "Wow! That really freaked me out!" leaving the person to struggle. We quite simply are not wired that way; we have to help if we can.

Imagine how good it would feel to save a life. Your self esteem would *have* to be flying high.

So it is with our teams. Again; never with the intent to manipulate, but understanding that people really want to help; we have to ask for it. Giving them an opportunity to help actually builds *their* self esteem.

Chapter Thirty Seven

Building Communication Bridges

Sometime during our one week Lean Leader workshop, we facilitate a *warm up* exercise we call *Building Bridges*. It is one of the most enjoyable exercises for me because it proves that we solve problems and work better as teams than we do as individuals.

We position a small table at the front of the room with a flip chart (or other barrier) hiding the table from everyone's view.

We then provide each team member team 10 Lego® pieces and tell them that they are going to build a lego bridge across the top of two soda cans separated by the distance of one soda can. They will have to build a free span bridge capable of holding a full can of soda without collapsing. There can be no upright supports and the bridge must not be attached to the support cans in any way.

There can be no talking, and only one person can approach the table at a time. No assignments are made about who goes first.

Participants may use one or more (up to all ten) of their Lego® blocks. If they retain any of their Lego® blocks, they are permitted to approach the table again and again. But once they have used all their blocks, they must remain seated.

Once all participants have applied their Legos® to the bridge, the screen is taken away and the facilitator places a full soda can on the bridge. In nearly every case the bridge collapses. And of course the team feels like they failed.

Illustration 37.1   Lego® building blocks

Then we give them a second chance. This time permitting them to work at their tables in small groups with the lines of communication open. Now they are able to come up with a winning solution; which in most cases involves turning the Lego's on *edge*, making a stronger joint.

Very few teams ever arrive at the solution when asked to work independently, as in the first iteration. When working without communication there may even be a team member who arrives at the solution on his or her own, but in nearly every case, someone else undoes it.

The value and importance of effective communication cannot be over emphasized. In school we are taught to solve problems on our own. We are trained to avoid solving problems with others.   It goes against our nature to work hard on our communication skills. As a manager, you will have your work cut out for you. However you choose to raise awareness of the need for effective communication among your teams, and whatever means you use to help them exercise and strengthen that capability, keep in mind that the strongest teams are made up of communicative individuals.

Chapter Thirty Eight

How many light bulbs does it take to change a company?

Light; we can't live without it.

It is the source of life on our planet. Light doesn't possess the normal properties that we generally associate with physical things; weight, shape or size. We can measure its speed and intensity, but we can't smell or taste it. We can feel and see its effects, and even store its energy for later use, but we cannot hold it with our hands. It is one of the most common and important aspects of the universe. But like gravity, light remains largely a mystery and many of its' properties defy clear explanation.

We've all heard the old joke, "How many psychologists does it take to change a light bulb?" (Answer: Just one, but the light bulb really has to want to change.)

I'd like to explore a similar question, by turning the puzzle around: "How many light bulbs does it take to change a company?"

Like many things, we may often take light for granted. We may even ignore it; that is, until it is no longer available. If you have ever walked into an unfamiliar room and are unable to find a light switch, you understand how dependent we have become on these little photon-generating devices that we call light bulbs.

A burned out light bulb can be very annoying, and in some cases create serious, even life threatening situations. So let's talk about the need to change the "old" bulbs—rooting out old ideas and methods in our companies and replacing them with new and modified procedures and polices, known collectively as the world-class manufacturing approach.

The analogy of the light bulb is here also meant to highlight that moment in a person's life when they recognize a new concept that just moments before lay hidden. The term most often associated with this experience is *epiphany*, which Webster's dictionary defines as "a sudden, intuitive perception of, or insight into reality; awareness of the essential meaning of something, often initiated by a simple, commonplace occurrence."

In lean manufacturing terms, it is the moment in which you are able to recognize the many forms waste (what the Japanese refer to as Muda) in your process; primarily wasted time, your only irreplaceable resource.

Non value-added activities cost time and therefore result in higher costs, longer delivery times, increased inventories, lower quality, and ultimately, fewer customers.

There are compelling reasons to ensure that more than one person in the organization recognizes the need to modify past practices. How many epiphanies does it take? How many mental light bulbs have to "come on" to change a company? We'll come back to that.

The Newest New Economy

There have been five major economic generations within the past 200 years:

- Steam (shipping by steam ship instead of sailing ships)

- Railroad

- Electric Motor

- Automobile

- Communication (Technology)

In each case, there were significant economic opportunities and growth in the early stages; lots of money being generated and circulated. In each case there was also economic downturns and even losses toward the maturation (or saturation) of each economic generation.

So the question, "What's next?" A better question might be, "If your company is world-class, why should it matter what's next?"

In any of the five primary economic generations just discussed, it would not have mattered if your business was a carpenter shop, machine shop, forging plant or hot dog stand. You would have benefited from the increased capital being infused into the economy during that moment in time.

As long as your company was viewed as a world-class provider of goods and services, you would have been a beneficiary of the economic growth.

It is reasonable to assume that you will also be able to supply to future economic generation as long as you maintain (or attain) world-class status during the current economic slump.

To be a viable supplier (then, now, or in the future), you have to satisfy three primary customer needs competitively, regardless of your era, geographic region, or economic generation: *timely delivery, exceptional quality, and acceptable costs.* In a nutshell, potential suppliers have to provide financial incentive for the customer to buy rather than make (or buy from a competitor). Ultimately, you must meet all three of these expectations while maintaining a reasonable profit margin.

The many tools of the lean manufacturing approach can help you meet these needs of the customer while improving your bottom line.

Our challenge is to learn everything we can about how other companies have applied these tools. It is time to explore the new behavioral technologies being applied by our competition.

There are hundreds of positive examples of organizations who have applied the lean approach. The key to sustainable change is that everyone in the organization must have the *epiphany* and commit to being what might be called a "light-bearer." There can be no dark silos in the organization where people can stand off with impunity; claiming no responsibility for taking action to support the lean efforts.

So the answer to the question "How many light bulbs does it take to change a company?" is easy: *every one.*

Chapter Thirty Nine

Ten Questions to Ask Yourself

In the journey to become a world class manufacturer, there are many tools to utilize; many techniques to apply; many terminologies to learn.

Please take time to answer each of the following ten questions. If you find a term unfamiliar, or if you have difficulty answering a particular question, it may suggest that an opportunity exists to educate yourself and your team about these terms, tools and techniques.

After asking the questions, we will define each term, and explain why each technique is critical when striving to implement a Lean transformation.

1. How many distinct value streams operate within your organization?

2. What percentage of your value streams have been value stream mapped?

3. What is the takt time for your primary value stream?

4. What is the value added ratio for your primary value stream?

5. What (%) reduction in machine set-up times (SMED) have you experienced?

6. To what degree has the 5-S program been implemented

7. What percentage of your facility is in cellular verse functional layout?

8. What is your current DPMO (six sigma metric)?

9. Are your kaizen events tied to clear and understandable business objectives?

10. What percentage of your materials (Raw, WIP, FGI) are replenished using a system known as kanban?

1. When companies first start up, they probably have a very small number of products or value streams. As the company expands, the growth leads to innumerable part types and the associated complexity. World class companies are discovering the value of simplifying; dividing the organization into smaller units called value streams. It permits the team to explore the improvement possibilities without being encumbered with the complex nature of the entire enterprise. It is not uncommon to see 12-15 product families flowing through 4-6 distinct value streams (some of which may be processed through the same machines or processes) within a company.

2. A value stream map is a visual representation of the processes required to produce a product or service. Because of the compounding effect of complexity caused by co-mingling multiple value streams it is nearly impossible to value stream map your entire company on one document. Step one is to identify the number of distinct value streams, and then map them individually. Later you can "roll-up" the data into one document if needed for overall plant capacity planning, loading

and line balancing, but separating them at the value stream level, and then mapping each stream is critical.

3. Takt Time is the manufacturing rhythm. Like the heartbeat provides a flow of blood in living creatures, the takt time fosters a flow of product through the processes. If one process produces more than the next operation can absorb, then problems occur. Everyone working to the same rhythm reduces inventory, waiting, motion, transportation, and all the other forms of waste. Takt time is calculated by dividing available time by demand. For example; a window manufacturing company produces two kinds of windows on two manufacturing lines; single pane picture windows, and double pane sliding windows. Lets say they work an eight (8) hour day (480 minutes available time) and they sell an average of 20 sliders per day and 30 picture windows per day, then the single pane window line would calculate their takt time as: 480/30 = 16 . Their takt time is 16 minutes per window. The slider team would need to produce a completed window every 24 minutes (480/20). Let's say that both teams share the glass cutting department. Because this department is a shared resource, it will have to produce at its' own takt time. Since sliding pane windows require two individual pieces of glass, the demand for glass is actually 70 per day. So their takt time might be expressed this way: 480/70 = 6.8 minutes.

4. A value added ratio is a fairly new concept to most people; it provides an indicator (metric) for companies seeking the lean approach. A ratio is express this way; 1:100 or 1:20. In this case, we are interested in finding the difference or ratio between value added time and non-value added time. Value added being defined as something the customer is willing to pay you to do

(e.g.: weld or paint). Non-value added is then; activities that the customer is unwilling to pay for (e.g.: moving product, counting, reworking defects, etc). The value added ratio provides an indication of how much time is spent working on a product verse how much time it spends sitting in a rack, or in someone's in-box, or in the warehouse. A value added ratio of 1:200 means that for every minute of value added activities, 200 minutes are spent sitting on shelf, or in a bin, or box, or any other non-value added process. World class companies are focusing on attaining a value added ratio of 1:10. Once your teams develop their value stream maps, it should be easy to calculate the true value added ratio of each value stream.

5. Like an Indianapolis 500 pit crew, Toyota has taught us the value of spending the minimum time in the pits as possible between production runs. Our machines are like race cars, and if we approach our change over like the pit crew does, we will find standardized ways of doing things to improve and reduce the downtime associated with set-up. SMED, or Single Minute Exchange of Dies clearly defines Toyota's method and goal of outpacing the competition. Recent developments in the automotive industry, proves that fast set-up is no longer optional. In over 250 set-up reduction projects we have found that a 50% reduction in machine downtime is nearly always possible. While not a typical result we have data showing that some teams have recognized as much as 92% reductions on the first try.

6. The 5-S program is one of the most visual and morale boosting techniques in which your teams can participate. Work place organization seems like common sense, but the 5-S disciplines take it to a new level. By first "Sorting" out what

243

you need and do not need, teams eliminate items that prohibit flow of material or information. Next "Straightening" up what they *do* need ensures that everything has a place, and that it is *kept* in its place. "Shine" has to do with the operator taking an active role in inspecting the machine through cleaning; making sure that the source of contamination is easy to identify because the machine is cleaned all the time. "Standardization" builds the techniques of Sorting-Straightening-and Shining into the work day. No more spring cleaning events; or end of the month clean up parties. The work area is cleaned throughout the day, every day; it is part of the standard work, and expectations are documented or made visual in other ways. "Sustain" is the hardest of the 5-S's, new habits are easy to break. For a while, there may have to be an audit process until the disciplines of 5-S become part of the organizational DNA.

7.   Most companies do not set out to develop wasteful manufacturing processes, it is an evolutionary process. When mom and pop shops start out, they arrange the first few machines they have into a small cell, each machine being positioned in the next logical step in the process. As new machines are added one at a time, they are generally grouped or arranged by function (i.e.: shears get grouped together with other shears, punching machines get grouped together with other punches). Over time, departmental (functional) layouts result in excess transportation between departments, layers of departmental supervision, excessive departmental inventories and departmental barriers. All manifesting itself in wasteful and time consuming job and material tracking; along with countless other non-value added activities. World class companies are working hard to restore the mom and pop shop

feel of cellular layouts within the larger organization; simplifying the layout; permitting each value stream to produce with the least number of departmental handoffs. Shared resources create challenges to this objective, but creative scheduling and hybrid takt times can net significant gains. Buying *right sized* equipment is another long term strategy toward this objective; thus avoiding the forced resource bottleneck associated with shared equipment.

8.   Another indicator of performance (in this case quality performance) is the DPMO or Defects per Million Opportunities metric. If your customer is not currently asking you for this dimension, get ready, they will probably soon begin seeking this metric as an indicator of your process capabilities. This Six Sigma technique does not mean that your team must become statisticians or mathematicians. The DPMO indicator is simply a method to magnify the quality of your output so that everyone has a common language. After examining water under a microscope, a water treatment technician might refer to a glass of drinking water as having a mercury contamination of 3.4 parts per million. That is a lot different than a contamination level of 3400 parts per million. As an example; let's say that US hospitals have a 99.9% success rate in giving the right baby to the right parents. That would do little to comfort the twelve parents going home with the wrong baby each day in America.

Hospitals have to get it right *more often* than that. Therefore many hospitals are using Six Sigma techniques and focusing on DPMO. By doing so, their goal is to reduce defects (mistakes) to zero. Six Sigma performance would permit only 3.4 mistakes out of a million opportunities.

9. Kaizen is a Japanese word for continuous improvement. To ensure that kaizen events are based on quality rather than quantity, steering teams should focus on making sure kaizen event charters are tied to a clear and communicated objective; objectives that are in turn, tied to the organizational vision. Make sure that a long term vision statement is connected to the short term deliverables being sought by the kaizen team.

10. When we go into a Mini-Market (like 7-11 or Circle K) there are really very few items on the shelf. The secret is the daily or weekly deliveries made by the dairy, bakery, soda bottlers and other suppliers. How many of the items that you use in the manufacture of your products are maintained on a "pull system" or kanban replenishment program. We can learn a lot by observing other industries, (i.e.: restaurants, gas stations, hotels, etc...) and how they manage their inventories. The goal is to have the minimum on hand while not putting customer deliveries at risk. The calculation for determining the proper amount to stock is as follows: Replenishment time divided by takt time.

Example: A glass manufacturer's supplier has a two week lead time for raw glass. Therefore: 2 weeks = 80 hours working time

80 hours = 4800 minutes.

If takt time is 6.8 minutes (as described above in item #3), then the replenishment signal must be sent before the inventory falls below 705 units.

$4800 / 6.8 = 705$

Of course this assumes that you know your takt time. Knowing your takt time also assumes that you have developed your value stream maps. This in turn assumes that you know how many value streams you have.

There are many additional tools in the Lean Manufacturing Toolbox. We explain many of them in our newly revised book "Lean Manufacturing for the Small Shop" published by SME.

World class athletes and sports teams spend the off seasons perfecting their skills and strategies for each upcoming season. We should do the same; US manufacturers should take advantage of the "breather" we have during economic slowdowns to prepare for the next wave of work that is sure to come.

It doesn't matter how good we were yesterday or last year or during the last economic boom. We have to get better everyday. Our customers have short memories of how good we were. They tend to be focused on how dependable and capable we will be tomorrow.

We hope that this short self examination might lead you to realize that your team must continue to educate themselves if they are to be viewed as world class in the future.

Chapter Forty

Lubbock Texas

As quality assurance manager for a precision sheet metal company, one of my responsibilities was to attend a monthly quality review meeting at one of our largest customers. Their Director of Quality and his staff of three were joined every month by five or six vender QA managers like me (from competing suppliers). We would meet for about an hour to discuss common quality concerns.

On one of my first visits, the Customer QA manager walked into the large conference room wearing a large button with the words *Lubbock Texas* on it. I thought he was proud of his hometown or something. Although it was very distractive, I determined that I would just not look directly at it.

About half way into the meeting, the conversation started to wander a bit, so I was taking some notes when everyone started laughing. I looked up to see what all the fuss was about, and the guy with the button was standing up, handing the button across the table to one of his co-workers; along with a hearty laugh.

I thought it was exceedingly odd. So I decided to ask them about it after the meeting.

They explained that one of the founders of their company had been a long-haul truck driver in his earlier life. On one trip to Amarillo, he and his driving partner were busy talking and missed their turn, ending up in Lubbock instead. As a technique to keep meetings on track, they use this method of redirecting their meetings in a non-threatening way. If you take the meeting off track, there is a good chance you will end up wearing the Lubbock button.

And don't you know; if *you* are the one wearing the button from the last meeting, you are very attentive to keeping the meeting on track, looking for any opportunity to remove the button and *give it away* to anyone who takes the meeting off track or down a rabbit trail.

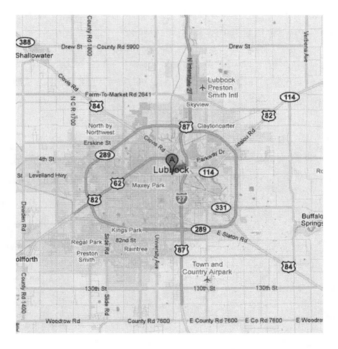

Illustration 40.1 Lubbock Texas, Source: Google Maps

The button served as a non-threatening, kind of fun but pointed method to keep meetings on track. The technique may not have worked for every company, but it seemed to work for them.

We must meet our teammates' *practical* needs. They are busy, and so we must use time effectively, keep focused on the key topics. We must effectively reach sound business decisions that everyone can support; having everyone feel that the team has met their objectives. This is a tall order, but with effective meeting facilitation, we can achieve these goals.

We must meet the *personal* needs of our teammates as well. They need to feel valued and respected. They need to feel that they were listened to. They need to feel that they have contributed to the discussion, and that they have shared in the development of meaningful solutions.

Having a meeting planned, with a published schedule including time limits assigned to each topic will go far to paint a picture of where the meeting should go; satisfying the requirement to meet practical needs.

Illustration 40.2   Parliament   Source: Word Press

Operating with the *polite disciplines of debate* (not like the interruptions and yelling you see between political and financial analysts or television coverage of the English Parliament) will help maintain each participant's self esteem and show respect for the personal needs of our team mates.

Chapter Forty-one

The Envelope Please

This short story comes from Las Vegas. A sheet metal company had just been acquired by a company in a completely different line of business. They thought that the addition of sheet metal fabrication would be a great addition to their thriving business model.

Illustration 41.1   Press brake

They quickly came to the painful realization that they did not know enough about sheet metal to make a smooth or profitable transition. I was brought in a bit too late. They were hemorrhaging quite severely, and their patience for undertaking a typical six week project (spread over 3-4 months) was not a financially attractive option. We took a very aggressive approach, using one product line as a model line; building a manufacturing cell that would capture about 40% of their business.

They had eleven press brakes (like the one pictured here). Our value stream analysis indicated that we needed six such machines (and operators) to sustain the current sales demand and we communicated such during our kaizen *report* to the management team.

The management team said we could have four.

The disbelief must have been apparent on my face.

I repeated the team's recommendation, "At the current takt time, and with the idea of minimizing overtime, the data shows that we actually need 6.2 machines, but we think we can improve scheduling and set-ups in order to maintain on time delivery with just six machines."

The General Manager played with his blackberry and without batting an eye; and without looking up, he repeated his earlier comment "You can have four."

The team schlepped back to the kaizen *war room* dragging their spirits and their tails on the ground. We were aware of the company's precarious financial position, and the old saying "You can't get blood out of a turnip!" seemed to be appropriate. But how on earth were we going to get six machines worth of work out of four?

It just happened to be lunch time, and instead of our usual routine of eating lunch together, the team decided that we all needed a break. We all went our separate ways for an hour.

I mindlessly drove to Taco Bell and sat in my rental car, quietly sipping on an ice tea and half heartedly chewing on a burrito supreme.

I thought to myself, "Man, taking this contract may have been a big mistake." In my 16 years of consulting I had never been a part of what I would have considered a failure. I had worked with companies that had struggled, but this seemed as close to an impossible task as I had ever faced.

I rejoined the team after lunch. I had never seen a more morose set of faces on any kaizen team. They were looking to me for an answer. I didn't have one. We sat in silence for a minute.

Then one of the kaizen team members offered a comment simply meant to define the hopeless situation in which we found ourselves. Inadvertently he provided us a light at the end of the predicament tunnel. He said "The only way to do six machines worth of work with four machines is to completely eliminate set-up; and that's not possible."

"Hold on now…" I said "How many parts; and how many set-ups are we talking about?" We had the value stream map hanging on the wall of the kaizen war room along with all the part prints.

"About 80 part types, a few slight variations, and four different material thicknesses." came the answer.

I asked the team; "So, if we are limited to only four machines, and if each machine could produce 25% (twenty of the eighty parts), is it possible to design a set-up on each machine that would allow an operator to produce any of the twenty parts on demand without a set-up?"

"That would be a stupid looking set-up" someone responded.

"What do you mean" I asked

"You would have to mix tooling. Straight punches and dies; gooseneck tooling, reversed and standard. You might even have to have a hemming die." The team looked at each other in silence for a moment.

"So you are saying that it might be possible?" I queried.

"It would be expensive to set it up the first time, and it may require that we buy a few duplicated tools so we don't have to share…but…yeah, it might work."

"How can we test it?" I asked

"Well, we have to sort these prints into four piles." The team members were all on their feet now; with renewed energy. They pulled the prints off the wall and within fifteen minutes had categorized them into four piles, determining that similar bend features could be performed together on certain machines and with similar tool configurations.

We set up a test and *within one day* the operators had developed four distinct; and in their own words; "stupid looking" set-ups on four machines. With minimal modifications they had found a way to process all the part types that they might see; virtually without set-up.

Having this kind of breakthrough would not have been possible if management had not challenged the team to the very edge of impossibility.

"The words 'Can't', and 'Won't, should be removed from our vocabulary." I have always repeated this phrase during kaizen training. If every time an idea is offered, someone shoots it down with a; "We can't do that!" or "They won't let us do that" or "We tried that before, that won't work!" then creativity is stifled.

I preach the need for *open-mindedness* everyday. And I have seen some amazing results by kaizen teams so I am rarely surprised, but in this case I was blown away by the solution the team came up with.

To get a 33% capacity improvement, a 33% reduction in required floor space, a $200,000 cost avoidance (the cost of two new machines) and a $60,000 ongoing labor cost reduction (annual) took my breath away.

It all happened because we were willing to listen to every comment, even one expressed out of frustration, and they were not afraid to *push the envelope*.

Chapter Forty-two

"I Need My Green Card"

I have never been a big fan of the term lean manufacturing; first it implies that the techniques apply primarily to the shop. For someone who spent years in the shop dealing with slow, inaccurate and redundant paperwork, I have always believed that continuous improvement should apply equally to the administrative functions and should often start in the office.

For the first ten years of my consulting career I spent 95% of my time conducting kaizen events in the manufacturing environment, but that began to change five or six years ago. Lately we spent about half of our time in the office, performing kaizen events within engineering, purchasing and other such administrative functions.

Even service businesses and governmental agencies are beginning to recognize the power of these tools and apply them in their organizations.

Such was the case in one Province of Canada. It was taking an average of fourteen weeks to process an immigration application. They would frequently lose a promising candidate to another country or province because the applicant might be seeking immigration to multiple countries at once.

While their province had many attractive reasons for applicants to seek work and residency, the "bird in the hand" principle often meant that they would cancel their application after receiving approval faster from Australia, Great Britain, United States or some other location.

In 2009, I was invited to train thirty administrators and staff members in an effort to reduce a fourteen week backlog (and lead time) to something approaching a few hours.

Illustration 42.1   Before condition 1,100 immigration files

We used the exact same tools we would use any manufacturing environment to reduce the process time, wait time, number of delays, reasons for work stoppage and other problems; value stream mapping, quality mapping, value added verse non-value added observations, set-up time and 5-S among others.

The results were breathtaking. Over a 50% reduction in number of applications in backlog (and they continue to reduce these every day).

Illustration 42.2 After condition 500 immigration files

In the *before* condition it required 46.4 minutes of labor per application for someone to perform data entry into the system when the application was straightforward and did not need a researcher to be involved. The same process now requires only 25.9 minutes; a 46% reduction.

When research was necessary (to validate college credits or similar tasks); it had historically required 36.6 minutes of additional effort. Through process simplification and standardization, it now requires only 9.8 minutes; another 73% reduction.

Prior to the event, over 70% of their files were taking fourteen weeks or longer to process; now that same 70% require less than four weeks.

They put a system of *triage* into place that grouped and assigned files based on examiner expertise. After one month, applications were moving so fast that they had to pay close attention to the payment system, because they were actually processing certificates before the check cleared. In a few cases they ended up sending out an applicants' certificate, and later the applicant check bounced.

Such experiences and the evidence behind hundreds of similar case studies convince us that the process of Lean works as well in administrative processes as well as it does in the shop. More and more companies who have adopted world class manufacturing principles in their shops are now realizing that the "Pull" on the office becomes unbearable. It often takes longer to process the paperwork than it does to actually manufacture the product.

This training project was so successful that recently the Minister of the Province invited me back to train another thirty managers and staff in their equivalent to our U.S. Dept. of Human Services.

This departments' goal is to provide wheel-chairs, medical care, legal or financial aid, and housing to physically; or mentally challenged Canadian citizens in a more timely and cost effective manner. This objective is now more possible than ever due to the training and efforts of these motivated administrators.

I encourage you to take a look at your administrative processes and add them to your strategic plan.

Chapter Forty-three

Russian Guard Story

I don't have a singular story of my own to go along with this, but it points out the need to challenge the current condition and not accept the current process as the only alternative. I am sure you will be able to use this story many time as I have.

In the mid 19th century (1860) Czar Alexander II of Russia had a visitor, German Prince, Baron Von Bismarck.

As the prince looked out a window in the palace he was admiring the beautiful courtyard. He couldn't help but notice a sentry stationed in the middle of the vast palace lawn.

Illustration 43.1   Russian Sentry   Source: Unknown

He asked the Czar why the guard was stationed there, not seeing an obvious purpose for his location.

The Czar could not recall exactly why the sentry was there; stating that to his recollection, there had always been a sentry at that location.

The Czar called in the Chief of staff, who also could not provide a satisfactory answer as to the reason a sentry would be stationed within a seemingly secure and enclosed courtyard.

Next the Commander General of the Armed forces was summoned. He did not know either, but he committed himself to find out.

Illustration 43.2 Daffodil   Source: Unknown

The investigation took three days. The Commander reported back to the Czar; "Eighty years ago Catherine the Great ordered the sentry," was the surprising answer.

It seems that one spring, Catherine the Great was looking out over this same courtyard on a beautiful spring morning. There was still snow on the ground, but a determined daffodil had pushed its way up through the bed of snow and thrown the most glorious yellow flowers toward the sun.

Catherine was so enamored with the flowers, and afraid someone would pick them that she ordered a sentry to guard the area to limit anyone's access to the blooms.

Of course a few weeks later the flowers wilted away. But the sentry remained. A few months later; and a few years later; and eighty years later the sentry was still there.

And if the German visitor had not asked the question, there may still have been a sentry standing there.

Totally non-value added.

We need to be willing to challenge everything we do and not only ask why, but also ask whether or not what we are doing is value added.

Chapter Forty-four

Staying off Track

As I write this the Discovery space shuttle is due to land at 11:57 AM in March 9th, 2011. This is the last scheduled flight of this particular space vehicle, and one of the last flights of the space shuttle program as well.

How many flights of the space shuttle program have there been? Discovery's last flight will be STS-133. One hundred thirty-three flights.

Illustration 44.1 STS133 Crew, Source: Nasa

John Glenn was on Space Transport Shuttle (STS) number 96. When I heard that fact about ten years ago, it surprised me. At the beginning of the space shuttle program there was enormous interest in each launch. People would travel for days to see a shuttle launch, but the overall level of interest seemed to wane after time. I would often ask workshop participants if the space shuttle was in space at the moment, seldom would anyone know.

Two horrific accidents would raise short-term awareness, but in the months that followed, people's attention waned again.

The new had worn off and it had become *normal*. Change is like that. Even though there is generally lots of attention paid to the roll-out of a new program or initiative like Lean; over time the newness will wear off and it will become the normal way of life.

Another reason to think about the space shuttle program and the accidents that happened is to remember and recognize how a small problem left unchecked can escalate into a major catastrophic failure.

In the case of the last space shuttle accident; it was evidently only a bit of moisture, that lead to a bit of ice forming and swelling behind some foam, causing a bit of foam to break off and fall; in the process striking a few tiles, leading to a bit of an overheating condition, which then lead on to a catastrophic meltdown upon re-entry to earth's atmosphere.

Evidently a number of people knew about each of these problems (relatively insignificant on their own), but either the people who knew, (or the people who needed to know) didn't want to risk being the bearer of bad news, (or declined to hear it).

While not trying to minimize the significance and loss resulting from that accident, we must avoid the risks of catastrophic failure of a program because we have overlooked the fundamentals. We cannot refuse to hear bad news either. We must invite and celebrate bad news, because it is an opportunity to get better.

Ok, too serious. Let's lighten this up a bit.

Here's something that you may not know about the Space Shuttle. The design engineers originally wanted the twin booster rockets to be larger (bigger in diameter). But part of the design process was determined by the transportation system used to move the booster housings. They would be shipped partially by train; their movement included a trip through a railroad tunnel.

The dimensions of railroad tunnels are determined in part by the railroad tracks themselves. The United States standard for railroad track spacing (distance between the rails) is 4 feet, 8.5 inches. Why?

Because European expatriates designed and built the US Railroads at the common European spacing of 4 feet 8.5 inches. Why?

Because European rail lines were built by the same people who built tramways; and tramways were built using the same jigs and tools used for building wagons.

Why did the wagons have that particular wheel spacing (4 foot 8.5 inches)? Because any other spacing, caused wagon wheel axels to break in established wheel ruts.

So who built those old rutted roads? Imperial Rome built the first roads throughout Europe.

Illustration 44.2   Chariot   Source: The Toy Man

What about the ruts in the roads? Well, Roman war chariots formed the initial ruts. Everyone else had to match the ruts or risk destroying their wagon wheels or axles.

Roman war chariots were just wide enough to for the back ends of two horses. So, a major design characteristic of the Space Shuttle; the world's most technologically advanced transportation system was determined over 2000 years ago by the width of a horse's behind.

So when we are examining a process; even though it may have worked for the past 50 years, we need to be willing to ask: "What horse's ass is responsible for this process?"

Just because someone laid down track (a process) years ago, does not mean it is the only possible means of accomplishing a task or reaching a destination.

Appendix

Now It's Your Turn

Just like the Chicken Soup for the Soul Series, I am convinced that there are many more stories out there that need to be told, and need to be heard. In fact, as I write this, I just remembered another great story I could add.

But I think I will save it for later.

In fact, I want to hear your stories too. There will soon be a follow up to this book.

Our next book will be called: **Catapult the Cow, Reloaded.**

I am inviting you to send us your story (or stories) for possible inclusion in the next edition. While there is no financial compensation for submitting a story, it should serve to build your network, expand the "body of *Lean* knowledge", and enhance your credibility, since your name as author will be included at the end of your story, as well as in the bibliography.

Your story can be of any length, but must be a *true* story. It must be of 5000 words or less, and in an MS Word or compatible (editable) format. High quality photographs are welcome, but if images include *identifiable* people, you must also include a release stating their permission for us to utilize their image.

Including *before and after* benefit analysis is always an effective teaching technique, please include data whenever available.

No proprietary company information (e.g.: customer names) or data may be included. The names of the company and individuals may be changed to protect their privacy, unless a written statement of permission is included.

A signed authorization by a company executive must accompany the submittal if actual company names are to be used. Keep in mind that case studies like this can serve as powerful marketing vehicles when companies are willing to share company name, logo, locations and other details. Individual team members can also be recognized by name, providing enormous morale boosting potential.

Editing may be performed at our discretion in an effort to maintain consistent style and continuity.

Send your electronic submissions to: Lean1mfg@aol.com

We will respond upon receipt of your submission, and you will be notified if your story is selected to be included in the next edition.

Illustrations and figures references and sources:

273

Mr. Gary Conner is an internationally recognized authority on the subject of Lean manufacturing.

Considered the Nobel Prize for manufacturing (by Business Week, magazine), Mr. Conner was awarded the Shingo Prize in 2002 for his work "Lean manufacturing for the Small Shop"; Published by SME (Society of Manufacturing Engineers). For a time, that text went on to outpace all other SME publications combined, becoming their best seller.

Author, consultant, trainer and kaizen facilitator, Mr. Conner has worked with over 150 companies, in 20 industries, facilitating over 500 kaizen events across the US and Canada.

Visit our website to obtain information about upcoming workshops, consulting services and other training materials.

Lean Enterprise Training

3530 N Coast Hwy

Newport, OR 97365

Email: lean1mfg@aol.com

Web: www.lean1mfg.com

Phone: 503-580-1156

ISBN: 1461065968